# THE
# POWER
# OF FIFTY
# BITS

# THE POWER OF FIFTY BITS

## The New Science of Turning Good Intentions into Positive Results

## BOB NEASE, PHD

**HARPER**
BUSINESS

*An Imprint of* HarperCollins*Publishers*

HarperCollins books may be purchased for educational, business, or sales promotional use. For information, please e-mail the Special Markets Department at SPsales@harpercollins.com.

FIRST EDITION

Designed by Renato Stanisic

Library of Congress Cataloging-in-Publication Data has been applied for.

ISBN: 978-0-06-240745-0

15 16 17 18 19   OV/RRD   10 9 8 7 6 5 4 3 2 1

For Delight and Addie

"Every body continues in its state of rest,
or of uniform motion in a right line,
unless it is compelled to change that
state by forces impressed upon it."

# Contents

# Foreword by Daniel Gilbert

**H**umans often make a mess of things. Those things include our relationships, our businesses, our finances, our health, and our planet. Our messes wouldn't be so puzzling if we didn't care, or if we didn't know any better. But we do, and we do. We *want* happy marriages and we *know* that philandering is a poor way to get them, but then we go off and do it anyway. We *want* carefree retirements and we *know* that saving money is the only way to get them, but somehow we just never get around to it. Instead of making choices that we know will behoove us, we make choices that leave us with no hooves at all. Why?

Philosophers, psychologists, and economists have spilled a lot of ink in the last few centuries trying to explain this puzzling tendency. Fortunately, Bob Nease isn't one of them. Rather, Bob is an engineer who, until recently (when he and his wife quit their jobs and moved to Italy to devote themselves to making wine), was the chief scientist at one of the world's largest pharmacy benefits management companies. His company had millions of members who were faced with choices about their own medical care, and Bob thought that his job was to help them make those choices intelligently. But when he tried to save them time and money, or when he tried to spare them worry and confusion, they often ignored his well-meaning attempts and sometimes even actively resisted them. Bob didn't want to explain this puzzling tendency. He wanted to fix it.

So Bob read all the books that the ink-spillers had written, and then started doing what engineers do best: tinkering. He designed programs and systems that used basic principles of human behavior to help his company's members make better decisions, and then tested those programs and systems in large-scale experiments. He kept the ones that worked, tweaked the ones that didn't, and then tested them again. And again.

Now, over the years, my tinkering has led to exactly one recipe for the perfect martini (combine frozen gin with absolutely nothing else ever) and a fairly reliable method for keeping the sous vide bag submerged in a pot of boiling water (hint: magnets). Bob's tinkering actually saved lives. As a result of his innovations, people who needed to take medicine took medicine. People who needed to get more exercise got more exercise. People who needed to see their doctors saw their doctors. And in the process of fixing the puzzling tendency, Bob developed a fascinating theory about where it came from in the first place. That's what this book is all about. In many ways, it is yet another one of Bob's cleverly engineered systems, expertly designed to hook you with an enigmatic title, hold you with delightful stories and deep ideas, and ultimately leave you better than you were before— wiser about people in general, and about yourself in particular.

In Italy, they toast with the word *salute*, which means "to health." It seems that Bob's work, Bob's book, and Bob's wine are all dedicated to the same basic proposition. I invite you to pour yourself a glass of *Fifty Bits*, sit back, and enjoy.

# Introduction

Several years ago, my wife, Gina, and I were in Atlanta
visiting some of her friends from the Centers for Disease
Control and Prevention. Gina has a PhD in epidemiology and
has worked on a variety of very challenging programs to improve public health. These initiatives include efforts to eradicate
polio in Nepal, HIV in Malawi, and sodium in my diet.

During our second night in Atlanta, a bunch of us went out
to dinner. Based on my past experience with the group, I knew
we'd be splitting the check. If you're a food lover like me, that
really complicates things. I love to eat, but because I knew that
the cost of whatever I ordered would be borne by everyone else
in the group, I needed to make sure I didn't get carried away. (I
wanted the shrimp carpaccio, the porcini flan, and the rib-eye
steak with horseradish whipped potatoes, but I realized that the
risotto and small green salad would be more prudent.)

This consideration was completely lost on another member of
the dinner party, a fellow whom I will call Jack. What I recall

most vividly about the evening was what Jack ordered. And ordered. And ordered some more. He drank faster than everyone else, treated himself to an appetizer and a salad, and chose one of the most expensive entrees. For dessert, he had crème brûlée and a cappuccino and finished off the dinner by ordering a snifter of port. I nearly jumped across the table.

I fumed in silence as my wife and I drove back to the hotel in our rented car. My fists gripped the steering wheel, my knuckles turned white, the vein in my forehead pulsed, and my jaw clinched. When Gina patted my shoulder and asked, "It's Jack, isn't it?" I nearly drove into oncoming traffic. No kidding, it's Jack. He'd been poorly behaved all night, single-handedly running up a tab that we would all have to pay.

## A FEW THINGS YOU SHOULD KNOW ABOUT ME

That dinner with Jack had a big impact in my professional life. To understand why, you need a little background about me. My undergraduate degree is in electrical engineering, and I come from a long line of clear-thinking, quantitative, and rational people. My father got his doctorate in electrical engineering from MIT and went on to become the chief scientist at Rockwell International (now Boeing); my mother had her bachelor's degree in education from Boston University. My grandmother on my mom's side was a teacher, my dad's father was adept at all things mechanical, and my dad's mother manipulated large numbers for fun—multiplying them, determining whether they were divisible by nine or eleven, assessing whether they were primes (or not)—all in her head.

I recently interviewed Steve Wozniak and joked that although we had a lot in common—fathers who were aerospace engineers, a love for science and practical jokes, facial hair, our beginnings in electrical engineering—somewhere along the line our paths had diverged (by several hundred million dollars, I imagine). He smiled and couldn't resist pointing out to a fellow engineer that he was still an exceptional circuit designer.

Me, well, not so much. The summer after I graduated from college, I worked at RCA in Burbank designing and building circuits for use in commercial movie projectors. On paper, I was a very bright engineer, but in practice, I was awful. The circuits I built worked only about half the time. I spent every day that summer sheepishly circling the parts supply station, eventually working up the nerve to ask the cranky guy behind the counter for more diodes and resistors and capacitors. But mostly transistors, which give up the ghost with a satisfying pop and a puff of white smoke when you hook them up wrong. The chief engineer at RCA didn't really like the idea of shipping theater equipment with more special effects than the films it was designed to project.

Fortunately, I'd already gotten into a master's program at Stanford University in a department that was then called Engineering-Economic Systems. The faculty was mostly comprised of electrical engineers who had escaped the chill of Boston's MIT and headed west to another type of chill altogether in the Bay Area of California. They applied systems engineering techniques to nontraditional problems. In practice, this meant more equations and computer models, and no circuits.

I loved it. The area that I found the most interesting was

something called *decision analysis*, which is a highly methodical and rational way to gain insight about what to do in the face of complexity, uncertainty, and dynamics. There was a bit of math involved, but I managed to mush through much of that, and fortunately the field was still new enough that a mediocre engineer like me could contribute a bit.

The Stanford approach to decision analysis had been developed by Ron Howard (not that one), a libertarian Buddhist electrical engineer from MIT. At the heart of decision analysis is the notion of an *ideal decision maker*—an imaginary person facing the same problem, having the same preferences, and in possession of the same information as a human decision maker. What makes the imaginary decision maker ideal is that, instead of using intuition and rules of thumb to decide what to do as humans do, the ideal decision maker uses logic and math to decide what to do.

In short, decision analysis is an engineer's perspective on classical economics. It takes as a given that people should be rational, and that they should make decisions that advance their own interests and preferences. Professor Howard's contribution was figuring out how to employ those principles for practical use in making important decisions. As one of his disciples, I spent the majority of my professional life promoting the application of decision analysis in health care and medicine. Until 2014, I was chief scientist at Express Scripts, a company that helps make the use of prescription drugs safer and more affordable by promoting the use of the most cost-effective medications and pharmacies. My work there involved researching the most effective pharmacy benefit designs (e.g., copayment levels) and developing tools to help patients make better decisions relating to how they used their prescription drugs.

In one evening, Jack changed all of that.

## HOW JACK CHANGED MY LIFE

Jack's bad behavior at that portentous dinner left me steaming well into the next day. I began to think about Jack's behavior in light of my doctoral training at Stanford. At the heart of things, decision analysis assumes that people should make decisions that are rational and that maximize their interests. Let's say that Jack ordered $50 more worth of food and drink than each of the rest of us did on average. Because there were ten people in our dinner party, his share would only be $5. That's a tenfold return on an investment with a payback period of about two and a half hours. It's the kind of performance that any CFO would applaud.

Two things struck me as I continued this line of thinking. First, Jack was the only one in our dinner party who had the nerve to act in his bald self-interest. Everyone *except* Jack had been much better behaved in terms of what they ordered. In sticking with the basic assumptions of decision analysis, Jack was the exception rather than the rule. It seemed as though everyone else was adhering to another set of unspoken behavioral principles.

This might not seem like such a big deal, but it was to me. Until that point, my Express Scripts colleagues and I had put a lot of effort into advising our clients (health plans, employers, labor unions, and the like) about how to apply financial incentives to encourage more cost-effective use of prescription medications.

For example, we recommended to our clients that they have the lowest copayments for generics and preferred brand medications, and higher copayments for more expensive medications. We also focused on making sure that patients knew that they could save money when they switched to an equally effective, lower-cost option—providing online tools and patient support teams to offer real-time cost comparisons between different medications. In short, we assumed that patients make decisions "by the numbers." Dinner with Jack, however, was a stark reminder that most of us make decisions—at least around the dinner table—based on something more than financial gain, logic, and pure self-interest.

In my role at Express Scripts, I knew that our own data showed that using financial incentives had an effect . . . but only a very modest one. I began to realize that we'd inadvertently and implicitly assumed that the majority of patients behave like Jack. If most people's behaviors and choices are influenced by something more than just financial incentives, then we shouldn't be surprised that strategies that relied on such incentives were only producing modest results.

The second lesson from my dinner with Jack was that trying to get people to make decisions "by the numbers" isn't just swimming upstream. It's fighting millions of years of evolution. Despite several years of very good education and training at one of the nation's best universities, my visceral response—the knee-jerk reaction that Jack's behavior was wrong—won hands down. My gut's reaction trumped any logical analysis. And if my own formal training as a decision analyst could be so easily swept aside by my wiring as a human, it seemed crazy to assume that others would behave any differently.

I began to seriously doubt whether demanding that people set aside their intuitions and instead embrace rational decision-making would ever have much of an effect on our day-to-day lives, including in health care. Instead, I wondered whether we would be better off reengineering the environments in which patients find themselves so that their natural inclinations lead to decisions and behaviors that better serve their interests over the longer term. This led my colleagues and me to develop a new approach to behavior that I call *fifty bits design*, and in the next chapter I'll explain more about what I mean. But for now it's worth pointing out how fifty bits design is different from other design approaches—namely, user-centered design. As you will soon see, fifty bits refers to a startling statistic: of the ten million bits of information our brains process each second, only fifty bits are devoted to conscious thought. This limitation means that, to a large degree, humans are wired for inattention and inertia, which in turn leads to a gap between what people really want (were they to stop and think about it) and what they do.

## FIFTY BITS DESIGN VERSUS USER-CENTERED DESIGN

User-centered design focuses on making things easy on the user. Websites battle over who can get the user what he or she wants with the fewest clicks. Call centers are judged by average time to answer and average handle time. The latest elevator systems use sophisticated algorithms to minimize waiting times.

User-centered design urges its practitioners to create interfaces that "get out of the way" and warns: "A user interface is like a joke. If you have to explain it, it's not that good." With user-centered design, the user is king (or queen), and the purpose of a system is to serve the user.

Fifty bits design is very different, and we'll go into the differences in greater depth in the last chapter of the book. For now, it's important to note that rather than start with what the user wants from the interaction, fifty bits design starts with what the designer wants from the user. Unlike user-centered design, fifty bits design assumes that users may not really know what they want, and even if they do, they might not put the effort into actively pursuing it. Fifty bits design assumes that much of the time, users' behavior is disconnected from what they'd want if they spent more time thinking about things.

User-centered design is agnostic. It assumes that the designer has no clue as to what's in the best interest of the user. It assumes that only the user knows; it advocates user involvement in the design process and focuses its energies on helping the users do whatever it is that they want to do. Because its focus is to "serve the needs of the user" as expressed by the user, user-centered design implicitly assumes that people are making choices rationally, deliberately, and in accordance with their own long-term interests. And that assumption is a major weakness that fifty bits design attempts to redress.

As I'll show in the rest of the book—and as all of us know from our own efforts and interactions with others—lots of behavior happens under the radar (i.e., without the benefit of careful, deliberate decision-making) and is driven by forces that were honed for a time long ago and a place far away. These natural inclinations were once adaptive, but they aren't necessarily adaptive for the world in which we currently live. We're exquisitely sensitive to losses, the group, and the present. Our attention—which requires use of one of the most energy-intensive organs in our bodies (namely, our brains)—is doled out sparingly.

At the core of fifty bits design is the hypothesis that bad choices don't spring from bad thinking, faulty information, or inadequate incentives. Instead, fifty bits design is built on the emerging understanding that most people have good intentions that remain latent, and thus focuses on strategies that activate those good intentions. Although this premise may seem counter-intuitive, even a brief reflection on our own situation and those of our co-workers, friends, and loved ones shows that it happens all the time.

## FROM GOOD INTENTIONS TO POSITIVE ACTIONS

Last year, Americans spent nearly $60 billion on diets and another $45 billion on exercise and fitness. The result? Two-thirds of American adults are still overweight or obese, and one-third of children are right behind them.

We're late changing the oil in our cars. We swear we won't wait until the last minute to do our taxes or turn in our term papers. We cement our intentions to get into shape by buying treadmills and elliptical machines . . . the majority of which wind up as clothes racks for the outfits we wish we could squeeze into.

The fact that people make lousy decisions and behave badly is old news. In a few short years, we have been tipped, blinked, nudged, switched, and swayed into admitting to ourselves and to others that we are more like Homer Simpson than we are like Mr. Spock. (Our parents and grandparents could have told us as much, and probably did, if we'd only been paying attention.) The question is no longer whether people are rational. The evidence is clear, the jury is in, and the bestseller lists have settled that question. We are *not*. The question is, now what? What practical solutions can marketers, human resource professionals, teachers, parents, and other real people use to improve behavior?

I wrote *The Power of Fifty Bits* to definitively answer that question.

My work at Express Scripts required me to distill the complex science of human behavior into a handful of principles that our thirty thousand employees could put into practice. In addition, I oversaw the implementation of those same simple principles into health-related programs that touch nearly a hundred million Americans.

*The Power of Fifty Bits* explains in simple terms how our brains—and thus many of our behaviors—reflect the instinctual and automatic systems that served us so well long ago and far away. More importantly, it will arm you with seven specific and proven strategies to improve behavior. Using accessible, entertaining, and relevant stories and examples, I've written *The Power of Fifty Bits* to be the world's first "how to" field guide that you can use to powerfully advantage better behavior for you, your loved ones, your co-workers, and your clients.

## BECOME A FIFTY BITS DESIGNER

The goal of this book is to help you to understand why we do what we do, and to equip you with practical tools and a set of principles that you can use to change behavior for the better. The seven strategies I lay out can be combined in numerous ways; as you master them, you will become an effective designer of better behavior. You will become a *fifty bits designer*.

To that end, the book is divided into three sections. The first section lays out the book's fundamental premise: people are wired for inattention and inertia. This specific insight leads to a much better understanding of why generally reasonable and well-meaning people engage in self-defeating behaviors. More importantly, it provides clear guidance about which strategies are likely to be more effective in changing behavior. It also provides an overview of the three key forces that shape nearly all of human behavior: how we react to losses, delays, and social expectations.

The second section of the book—chapters 3 through 9—focuses on seven powerful and practical strategies for dealing with human inattention and inertia. In many ways, this section is the meat of the book. It's written to provide a working understanding of each of the seven strategies.

Chapter 10 closes out the book. It opens with a compelling example of an organization that combined multiple fifty bits strategies to profoundly change an important health-related behavior. Because organizations could use these seven strategies to advantage behaviors that are in their interest but not in the interest of those whose behaviors they are trying to change, I provide some guideposts to help avoid these temptations. This chapter also includes thoughts about the implications of fifty bits design for digital interactions and "big data." It closes with a few final thoughts about what makes fifty bits design different and superior to competing approaches.

Many of the examples in *The Power of Fifty Bits* show how to apply the seven strategies in the health and wellness setting. I've adopted this lens for two reasons. First, I have spent nearly all my professional career focused on ways to help people make better medical decisions. This area of work started when I was a graduate student at Stanford and continued when I was an assistant professor of community and family medicine (under the guidance of Hal Sox and Jack Wennberg) at Dartmouth Medical School and then an associate professor of internal medicine at Washington University in St. Louis. My work took a much more practical turn over the past thirteen years at Express Scripts. Health-related decisions and behaviors is an area to which I have given a lot of thought.

Second, based on my work at Express Scripts, it's clear that behavior is a critical "rate limiter" in health care. We eat, drink, and smoke too much; we exercise and sleep too little. We do a poor job of taking our medications as prescribed, and we all too frequently skip a handful of tests proven effective in reducing our chances of really nasty outcomes (e.g., heart attacks, stroke, colon cancer). There are lots of opportunities for better outcomes if we can improve health-related behaviors.

Despite the focus on health care, however, the solutions in the book can be applied in a number of settings. The insights and solutions put forth in *Fifty Bits* are essentially about human brains and behavior. The same brains that lead to health-related behavioral hiccups inevitably lead to hiccups in other settings. Approaches effective in activating better health behaviors are equally effective for improving other behaviors as well.

. . . .

**That dinner with** Jack so many years ago precipitated a change in my thinking about how to improve the choices and behaviors of millions and millions of Americans and profoundly reshaped my work. But for Jack's selfish, blood-boiling behavior, I might never have discovered how important inattention and inertia are when it comes to human behavior, and I might never have devoted years of intense work to uncover the seven strategies you're about to learn. So Jack, wherever you are, I forgive you. And the next time we go out to dinner, I'm buying.

# THE
# POWER
# OF FIFTY
# BITS

# CHAPTER 1

# Wired for Inattention
# and Inertia

In the week before Easter of 1889, President Benjamin Harrison appointed Robert P. Porter to the post of supervisor of the census. Porter immediately faced a nightmare of constitutional proportions. Normally, such an appointment would be an honor, but Mr. Porter found himself with an immediate headache. Article 1, Section 2 of the US Constitution mandates that a census be taken every ten years. Unfortunately, the previous census of 1880 had taken nearly a decade to complete and was just barely rolling off the presses when Porter took on his new job. Because the population of the United States had continued its upward climb, the best guess at the time was that the 1890 census would take thirteen years to complete—which would obviously create a big complication come time for the 1900 census. Mr. Porter was in a pickle.

Fortunately, an electromechanical whiz kid named Herman Hollerith was already all over the problem. At age nineteen, Hollerith had worked on the 1880 census and had a firsthand appreciation of both the size and the nature of the challenge. In fact, Hollerith had anticipated the problem years earlier and had developed a system that he believed would dramatically shorten the time required to complete the census.

Hollerith's key insight was that the choke point for the US census was not the collection of the data—done by enumerators going door to door—but the speed at which the data they'd collected could be processed. Prior approaches involved tabulating and sorting data by hand, tracking counts with tally sheets and a series of hash marks (in groups of five).

Hollerith cracked the nut by employing punch cards that could be quickly "read" using an electromechanical system of metal pins that poked through the punched holes and into wells filled with mercury. This completed a circuit and incremented a series of forty counters that kept track of age, household status, employment, race, and a number of other variables captured for the census. Hollerith's automated system was far faster than the approaches that came before; the rough population count was complete in a matter of months, and the full tabulation (which was far more robust than previous analyses) was completed with plenty of time to spare. Hollerith's machine served as a launching point for applications in other areas, and the company he founded eventually became International Business Machines— known today as IBM.

The human brain has its own processing choke point. Each second, your brain devours about ten million bits of information. This is the equivalent of having the original Ethernet cable running at full capacity plugged directly into your brain. The hang-up is that the conscious part of your brain (and mine as well)—the part of the brain of which we're aware when we're using it—can only process about fifty bits per second.

This is a stunning pair of information-processing rates, because it shows us just how scarce human attention is. If you doubt how limited your attention really is, try simultaneously singing "The Star-Spangled Banner" and counting backward from 100. Or make yourself aware of the way the chair feels on your rump, and the sound of whatever is going on around you, and then spell "cantaloupe" backward . . . all at the same time. Most of us can't, and we shouldn't take it personally.

I'm not sure what's more difficult: to appreciate how fast ten million bits per second is, or how slow fifty bits per second is. But here's a way of wrapping your mind around how slow your mind is wrapping itself around things. Let's assume that a cup of sugar represents all the information entering your brain each second. In this scenario, the part your conscious mind is aware of is about ten grains—an almost undetectable amount. In short, 99.9995 percent of our bandwidth is beyond the reach of our awareness.

## THE INTENT-BEHAVIOR GAP

The fundamental idea of *The Power of Fifty Bits* is that for better or worse our brains are wired for inattention and inertia, not for attention and choice. This point is critical for those of us who are trying to improve behavior, because most of the time we act as though people have an infinite appetite for information and a boundless willingness to make decisions. Nothing could be further from the truth.

The fact of the matter is that we tend to focus our attention on things that are either pressing or pleasurable. Life—what happens, as John Lennon sang, when we are busy making other plans—is loaded with mundane stuff that is neither pressing nor pleasurable. That means we pay little attention to much of what we do. If the status quo isn't painfully broken, and if an alternative doesn't tickle our fancy, we are apt to let things ride.

Once you understand it, you begin to see evidence of the intent-behavior gap all around you. When I was at Express Scripts, we partnered with a national survey firm to estimate the size of the intent-behavior gap for key medication behaviors. To do this, in the first half of the survey we asked respondents whether they were using brand-name or generic medications, whether they were using home delivery or retail for their maintenance medications, and which retail pharmacies they were using. (In each of these cases, one option is lower cost and offers equal benefits: using a generic rather than a brand, having long-term medications delivered directly to your home rather than going to a retail pharmacy, and using the lowest-cost retail pharmacies for short-term medications.)

Later in the survey, we presented respondents with realistic pairs of options (e.g., getting their long-term medications by home delivery instead of going to a retail pharmacy). This approach allowed us to determine the fraction of people who were doing one thing (e.g., using retail pharmacy for their long-term medications) but who preferred something different (e.g., home delivery) when they stopped long enough to think about it. Eight of ten users of brand-name drugs would rather be on a generic, seven out of ten people getting their medications in retail would rather be getting their long-term medications in home delivery, and four of ten users were willing to move to a different retail pharmacy if it saved their plan money . . . even if it didn't save them any money in the near term. (The seven-out-of-ten statistic for home delivery reflected copayments that were very favorable for mail order; it dropped to five out of ten for copayments that are more typical.)

The intent-behavior gap is critical because it radically alters how we approach behavior change. Human resource executives, marketers, and others often infer people's underlying intentions from observed behaviors (e.g., most patients are getting their maintenance medications from retail pharmacies, so they must prefer retail over home delivery). This leads us to focus on strategies for changing underlying intentions—strategies that focus on persuasion, cajoling, and the like.

The intent-behavior gap tells us that when we use these approaches we are very likely barking up the wrong tree. It's no wonder that we are routinely disappointed by educational campaigns aimed at extolling the virtues of this behavior or that, or by financial incentive schemes to lure people into the desired behavior. These things have less effect than you'd guess because *lots of people already believe in the virtue and value of the behaviors that are being promoted.* The problem isn't that people's intentions are pointed in the wrong direction. It's that people are not acting on the good intentions that they already have.

The intent-behavior gap is at the heart of some extremely powerful solutions for changing behavior. We don't need to change people's intentions. We don't need to persuade them or to attempt to change their minds. What we need is to activate their preexisting intentions to do the right thing.

Adherence to medications provides an interesting example of how a "fifty bits" point of view significantly changed our approach. If behavior and intentions move in lockstep, and you observe that patients aren't taking their medications as prescribed, then you must conclude that their behavior is deliberate: patients aren't taking their medications because they think the drugs aren't working, or are causing side effects, or cost too much. As a result, the solutions you design will focus on solving these problems (e.g., lowering the cost of medications).

But when you look at nonadherence through the lens of fifty bits, an entirely different set of causes rises to the top, and these lead to very different solutions. We should expect a lot of forgetting and procrastinating by patients: forgetting to take their medications, delays in getting refills, and delays in getting new prescriptions when they have no more refills left. Fifty bits tells us that nonadherence will be accidental rather than deliberate.

This situation is exactly what my colleagues and I found when we looked at patients taking medications for high blood pressure: nearly 70 percent of nonadherence was completely accidental—patients periodically forgetting or procrastinating on refills and renewals. The remaining causes for nonadherence were equally split between cost concerns and clinical concerns. When you ignore the fifty bits limitation, you risk losing sight of an entire class of causes of suboptimal behavior, and you fail to pursue effective solutions for those problems.

Once you understand and believe in the fifty bits way of looking at the world, a lot changes. You stop focusing on trying to change behavior by changing intentions. Instead, you start focusing on strategies that activate the good intentions that already exist for most people.

## OUR LAGGY, LAZY BRAINS

Inattention and inertia reflect the way human brains are wired, and that wiring is a reflection of the way our brains evolved. Like any other organ, our brains are the result of millions of years of evolution. (If you're the parent of a teenager, you'll probably want to take evolution aside for a very stern discussion and ask whether this is really the best that could be done with such a generous timeline.)

That our brains are evolved organs leads to two critical and interlocking insights. The first is that they are stuck far in the past. For the vast majority of our evolutionary history, we've lived in small groups scraping by, foraging plants and hunting animals. It's an existence that the evolutionary psychologists Leda Cosmides and John Tooby describe as "a camping trip that lasted an entire lifetime," and it's been that way for millions of years.

If you doubt that our brains are stuck in the past, just consider the things that spook us. For example, many of us fear spiders and snakes, and why not? They're creepy, and as we all know, they can be deadly. But a cool-headed look at the data shows that our fears are wildly overblown. In the United States, snakebites cause five to seven deaths per year, and deaths from spiders are so rare that it's tough to get a reliable estimate of the risk (there were only two reported deaths from spider bites between 2001 and 2005). In contrast, every year six hundred or so Americans suffer bicycle-associated deaths, and about six hundred thousand Americans die each year from heart disease. If our fear circuits were calibrated to today's environment, we would be about a hundred times more skittish about ten-speeds than rattlesnakes, and completely petrified of cigarettes and saturated fats.

It's not just about fear. We're wired to solve all sorts of problems that we faced way back when and way over there—problems that, for the most part, we no longer face. Conversely, we now face daily tasks (e.g., shopping for food, deciding whether to go to a movie or stay home and read) that were nonexistent for our ancestors.

In other words, evolution has endowed us with a set of mental capabilities and functions that are solutions to key problems—but they are the problems faced by our ancestors over vast periods of time in our long-ago past. Our species spent nearly its entire existence in a relatively stable and harsh environment, and it's in that environment where natural selection has done the majority of its work. Ten million years is a length of time that's incomprehensible to most of us, and try as we might, it's simply impossible to grasp how narrow the time window is in which we've made some of our most important advances—including ATMs and microwave popcorn.

But perhaps even more germane is how radically our environment has changed in our very recent past. Our standard of living was stuck in the mud for nearly all of human history. This situation has improved dramatically—at least in developed countries—since the dawn of the industrial revolution only about three hundred years ago. Until that time, we were held in a tight Malthusian, zero-sum grip: the only way for me to do better was for you (or someone else) to do worse; increases in the quality and length of life for some people only occurred by offsetting decreases in the quality and length of life among others. Sadly, wars and plagues improved the lives of those who survived them because a fixed set of resources was available to a smaller number of people.

And then something remarkable happened. The industrial revolution produced a rising tide that for the first time in the history of humankind lifted all boats. No longer were improvements in quality of life in one group dependent on increased misery among another. It was as if, at least among a large chunk of the world's population, the rules of the game changed dramatically.

Why does this matter? Because this major shift happened in a time frame so recent that evolution has not had a chance to catch up. In a very real sense, our brains—and the instincts, sentiments, and inclinations they produce—are living fossils from a very different environment.

## PREDICTABLY IRRATIONAL OR LIVING LOGICALLY?

The realization that human inclinations and instincts are a peek into the past can help resolve the ongoing tension that exists between classical economists and social psychologists. Traditional economists argue that people are mostly rational and that they reliably respond to incentives (often referred to as the *Homo economicus* model). Psychologists often focus instead on how irrational people are and how they reliably violate the assumptions of classical economics (affectionately referred to as *Homer economicus* in a nod to the donut-loving father from the television show, *The Simpsons*).

Economist and journalist Tim Harford, for example, has observed that as the cost of unprotected vaginal sex increases (e.g., by decreasing the availability of abortions or requiring parental notification), rates of sexually transmitted infection among teenagers (relative to those for adults) drop, presumably due to less frequent sex or greater use of condoms. This shift is precisely the effect one would predict if teens were making decisions about sexual behaviors in a rational manner: as costs increase, demand decreases.

Psychologists, on the other hand, have convincingly argued that people reliably deviate from rational decision-making. In the same arena of sexual behavior, for example, social psychologist Dan Ariely notes that people not only make different decisions when they are sexually stimulated than when they are not, but they also incorrectly predict that they will behave the same in both aroused and unaroused states. This "hot state/cool state" effect is difficult to fit squarely within a rational model of decision-making.

Harford celebrates the rationality of people engaging in everyday behaviors (the trick is to understand the incentives to which people are responding), while Ariely relishes the predictable irrationality of those same people. So which is it? Are people reliably rational or predictably irrational?

As interesting as these arguments are, they obscure a more fundamental point. The question isn't so much whether people are rational or irrational. The fifty bits perspective says that most of the time we're neither. Instead, a more useful distinction is to think about whether our behaviors are *adaptive* or *maladaptive* to the current environment. Those behaviors that are adaptive appear to be rational; those that are not adaptive often appear to be irrational. For example, most of us enjoy eating foods that contain fat or sugar (or both), and we may find that at times we eat a lot more than we should. This behavior doesn't make a lot of sense, because after engaging in it we experience regret and may even devote additional time and effort to undo the results of our behavior (e.g., diet or exercise). But in the resource-scarce environment in which our brains developed, this sort of behavior would have been very adaptive: eating foods high in calories (i.e., containing fat or sugar) and consuming past the point of comfort would offer evolutionary advantages.

Rationality may simply be a by-product of (mostly automatic) behaviors shaped by past natural selection that still happen to work well today. Mother Nature is the ultimate pragmatist. What works is what matters; rationality or irrationality has little to do with it.

## HOW TO BEHAVE ON 1,200 CALORIES A DAY

Because our brains are stuck in the faraway past, they are honed to solve the key problems they faced way back when. To better understand why we do what we do, it's useful to consider what life was like for our ancestors.

Cosmides and Tooby's description of our past environment as a "camping trip that lasted an entire lifetime" might be overdoing it just a bit, and by this I mean that most of my camping trips would be extremely cushy by comparison. You say "camping trip" and I immediately think of a Coleman stove, a tricked-out tent, provisions for s'mores, and lots of goodies and gadgets picked up from REI on the way out of town in my SUV. A camping trip for me means a lot of driving, a little hiking, plenty of swatting at mosquitoes, and furtive Googling of nearby up-scale hotels on my iPhone. But back then, where our brains grew up, most of our waking hours were spent scrounging up something to eat, or trying to avoid being eaten.

As any good physiologist, astute viewer of *Survivor*, or parent of teenagers knows, things can go very bad very quickly when you don't have enough calories on hand. Your brain consumes about 20 watts of power to operate. In terms of lightbulbs, that's not particularly bright, so I'd advise against trying to impress a date with that figure. But in relative terms, it's quite a bit. In fact, your brain is one of the most energy-intensive organs in your body. It accounts for about 2 percent of your body weight but uses about 15 percent of your cardiac output (the blood flowing from your heart), 20 percent of your total body oxygen, and 25 percent of your blood sugar. That's about 450 calories every day.

It's theoretically possible that our brains could use even more energy, but probably not without getting bigger. And if the challenge posed by a larger head is lost on you, I'd wager that you've never given birth vaginally. Bigger heads mean more difficult deliveries, and as women who've been there can tell you, the current size of a baby's head is quite big enough, thank you very much.

To top it off, because our brains have no way to store energy (e.g., fat), they need a quick source of fuel, and that turns out to be glucose—blood sugar. This means that extra activities on the part of the brain can deplete accessible fuel surprisingly fast; energy available for our brains runs at a premium. In short, because the brain has no way to store energy for a rainy day, it runs a tight ship.

So what's an energy-hungry brain like yours doing in such a calorie-restricted environment? Looking for a snack, probably. But one thing of which we can be certain is that your brain is not about to waste precious and expensive brainpower in situations in which less expensive shortcuts will do.

Our brains are constantly relying on heuristics—or simplified rules of thumb—to get the job done as efficiently as possible and without engaging our scarce fifty bits. For example, in estimating distance, our visual processing system relies on haze;

the hazier something is, the farther away it appears. This hazier-means-farther-away shortcut is a good rule of thumb because all else being equal, haze and distance go together: the farther the light reflecting off that distant object has to travel, the more scattering will occur. But the heuristic breaks down when there's more stuff than usual hanging around in the air (e.g., fog)—haze goes up but the distance does not. That's one of the reasons pilots learn to fly by instruments during bad weather.

The simple rules of thumb that our brains use are great when they work—they're fast and cheap. But there's no free lunch: shortcuts honed in our ancestors' past can lead us astray when applied today. For example, researchers wondered whether lighting played a role in whether people behaved honestly when they had the chance to cheat, and they found that participants were more likely to cheat on self-rated exams when the room was dimly lit. This isn't necessarily surprising, because all else being equal, the chance of getting caught cheating decreases as it gets harder for someone to see us doing it.

But the results from a second experiment were a bit more surprising. In that experiment, half the subjects wore tinted glasses while the other half wore nontinted glasses. Subjects in both groups solved math problems, graded their own performance in secret, and paid themselves based on that performance, all on the honor system. That is, the chance of getting caught cheating for anyone in the study was zero, regardless of whether the glasses worn were tinted or not. Nonetheless, subjects wearing the tinted glasses were more likely to cheat than those in the control group.

That's right: wearing tinted glasses caused people to cheat more than they would otherwise. From a logic standpoint, this makes about as much sense as a little kid who covers his eyes and squeals, "You can't see me!" But from the perspective of a lazy brain, it makes a lot more sense. Over time our brains have come to associate darkness with a looser attitude about cutting corners. The rule "If it looks dark, you can probably get away with things" works well in an environment in which the only way things looked darker to us was if we were in actual darkness.

But that rule of thumb didn't (and couldn't) anticipate a situation in which our own eyes would be looking in the dark but everyone around us would be seeing in the light. That situation just didn't exist naturally. The "It's okay to cheat a bit if it's dark" rule worked well because the environment in which the rule emerged never involved a situation in which the person considering cheating would be in the dark but those who might catch him were not. And this explains why subjects wearing tinted glasses cheat more than those wearing clear glasses, and why there is very little cheating when the lights are on, even if there is full assurance that one will not get caught.

There's a subtle but very important lesson here. In the case of cheating, our underlying cognitive machinery doesn't waste time or energy calculating the actual chances of getting caught; that's just too expensive. Instead, we're wired to loosen up on the ethical behavior more in the dark because that's what generally tends to work—or at least it did so in the past. So here's the lesson: the rational part of things (i.e., that darkness offers a cover for bad behavior) explains *why* this rule of thumb works generally. But if a rule of thumb works well long enough, it becomes part of human nature and remains there even if the underlying logic no longer applies.

## BRAINS ON AUTOPILOT

As noted, each of us has only fifty bits per second of conscious bandwidth to guide our behaviors; the rest happens automatically. For control freaks like my wife, the thought that a large part of behavior happens below the radar and outside of our reach is truly terrifying. For the rest of us, the fact that our unconscious brains could be doing a bunch of hard work while our conscious minds are watching TV seems almost too good to be true. Either way, it turns out that our conscious minds really have no idea how those choices are being made, or why. The psychological literature is awash with interesting examples of this reality, but I will share just a couple of them.

Several studies have shown a small but real relationship between people's names and decisions they make. For example, people are slightly more likely to work at companies whose names share the first initial of their own last names. One study estimated that about twelve thousand Belgians work where they do because of this effect. Similarly, people named Dennis are slightly more likely to become dentists; people named Louis are slightly more likely to live in St. Louis.

There are dozens of studies of how priming—gentle nudges in one direction or another of which subjects are not consciously aware—can alter people's choices. People who are made to feel hungry are less likely to donate money to charity, and people who are made to feel poor are more likely to consume extra calories. In the setting of health care, we found that people who were primed to think about their place in the local community showed greater attachment to their local pharmacy and less attachment to big chain pharmacies.

The point here is not so much that these effects exist, although they are pretty interesting in and of themselves. The point is that if you ask people directly what went into their decisions about what they do for a living, where they do it, charitable giving, eating habits, which medications they take, or where they get those medications, precisely none of the above-noted factors will be mentioned. And the reason they won't be mentioned is because our subconscious brains don't see fit to share those details with our conscious minds. As the neuroscientist David Eagleman puts it in his book *Incognito: The Secret Lives of the Brain*:

> The first thing we learn from studying our own [brain] circuitry is a simple lesson: most of what we do and think and feel is not under our conscious control. The vast jungles of neurons operate their own programs. The conscious you—the I that flickers to life when you wake up in the morning—is the smallest bit of what's transpiring in your brain. Although we are dependent on the functioning of the brain for our inner lives, it runs its own show. Most of its operations are above the security clearance of the conscious mind. The I simply has no right of entry.

That the conscious mind lacks the proper "security clearance" to access the part of the brain that's calling a lot of the shots has important implications for things like focus groups and user surveys. The results of these types of investigations should be interpreted very, very carefully. Any time we start asking people why they do or don't do this, or why they like or don't like that, we are only getting the fifty bits version of reality. We are not getting the whole story—not even close.

**In this chapter,** we've seen that people are wired for inattention and inertia—that's the fifty bits challenge. Together, inattention and inertia frequently cause overt behaviors to become unhooked from our best intentions: what we do drifts away from what we want to do. This situation happens not because we're flawed but instead because our brains were honed for an environment that in many ways was much different than the environment in which we live today.

The promise of this book is to empower you with a set of strategies that close the gap between what people want to do and what they really do by activating the good intentions that most of us already have. But before we look into those strategies, it's helpful to better understand the three most powerful shortcuts that people use. In fact, these shortcuts are so strong and pervasive that they can be thought of as behavioral forces. As we'll see, the seven strategies are always informed by, and often leverage, these forces.

# CHAPTER 2

# Behavioral Shortcuts

When I was about eight years old, my family took a vacation to Yosemite National Park in the Sierra Nevada mountain range. Like most kids whose parents carefully plan vacations to expand their horizons and provide an educational experience, I remember almost none of it. I do remember a giant sequoia so big a tunnel had been carved through its trunk, big enough for our station wagon to drive through. I also remember a display of a complete cross section of a much smaller but still enormous sequoia that had been turned on its side so visitors could get a good look at all of the rings. Fifteen hundred years of history—from well before the Battle of Hastings to the US Civil War and beyond—was laid out before me, captured by the rings that trees form in their annual growth cycles.

Just as those old sequoias have within them the marks of ages past, so too our brains carry evidence of the environment in which we emerged as a species. As we saw in the previous chapter, that environment was uncertain and dangerous. To survive, our ancestors banded together in groups, which provided better protection and allowed for division of labor and other benefits. As a result, many of our behaviors today reflect three shortcuts that worked well in the past. Understanding these shortcuts will help us build strategies for unlocking good intentions today.

## SHORTCUT #1: FIT IN

In the spring of 2006, Comedy Central aired an episode of *South Park* entitled "Smug Alert!" The episode suggested that owners of hybrid cars tend to exhibit a sense of superiority over those who drive gasoline-guzzling, emissions-burping alternatives. In it, Gerald Broflovski (Kyle's dad) buys a "Toyonda Pious" and proudly flies his environmental flag by driving it everywhere and demanding attention. Gerald soon starts a campaign to get the other folks in South Park to switch to the Pious as well. His plan works, but by the time Gerald prevails, his close friends can't tolerate his attitude. The Broflovskis then move to San Francisco to join other like-minded people. Soon both South Park and San Francisco are enveloped in a gigantic cloud of "smug"—the result of high-profile environmentalists spewing "self-satisfied garbage" into the atmosphere. As a result of all this smug, all of the cars of South Park are destroyed.

The irony is that in the year following the broadcast of this *South Park* episode, sales of the Toyota Prius went through the roof. And a couple of subsequent studies confirmed the creators of *South Park*'s intuitions about why people were buying the cars. The *New York Times* reported that by the second quarter of 2007, 57 percent of people buying a Prius said the main reason for their purchase was that "it made a statement about me."

Indeed, the *Times* quoted a couple of people who were quite transparent about their motives for buying a Prius:

> "I really want people to know that I care about the environment," said Joy Feasley of Philadelphia, owner of a green Prius . . . "I felt the Camry Hybrid was too subtle for the message I wanted to put out there," Ms. [Mary] Gatch said. "I wanted to have the biggest impact that I could, and the Prius puts out a clearer message."

Most economists look at hard data rather than warm fuzzies when trying to figure out what's driving purchasing decisions. The economists Alison and Steven Sexton were able to tease out the market share of Prius sales that were due to the green "halo" effect associated with that car. To do that, the Sextons used the natural geographic variation in environmental conscientiousness coupled with the fact that other hybrids were available that were as environmentally friendly as the Prius but less obvious in terms of the look of the car.

Here's how their analysis worked. The researchers examined voter registrations and election results in the states of Washington and Colorado. These are good states at which to look, because of the geographic variation in the fraction of people who "lean green" environmentally. For example, the city of Boulder, Colorado, is part of Boulder County, and in the 2012 presidential election voters there went for Obama over Romney (69.6 percent to 28.0 percent). In contrast, the city of Greeley is in Weld County, and voters there went for Romney over Obama (55.3 percent to 42.1 percent).

Because people who vote for Democrats generally place greater value on the environment than do people who vote for Republicans, the researchers made two predictions about the purchases of hybrid vehicles. First, and pretty obviously, more hybrid cars would be sold in areas with more Democrats. Second, and less obviously, if people are buying Prius hybrids to signal their environmental "cred," the Prius market share among hybrids would be higher in areas with more Democrats. In other words, left-leaning towns should have not only more hybrids but more *conspicuous* hybrids. That's because the signal that the Prius sends is more valuable in a town in which environmental friendliness is more valued.

And that's precisely what the Sextons found. They concluded that "conspicuous conservation" accounted for about one-third of Prius market share in Colorado and about one-tenth of the market share in Washington. They also estimated that the dollar value placed on the "green halo" associated with the Prius was about $1,000 in Washington and closer to $3,300 in Colorado.

Trey Parker and Matt Stone, creators of *South Park*, had their fingers on the pulse of this part of human nature. It seems as though even with decent alternatives for reducing gasoline use associated with driving, some people can't help signaling where they stand on the environment—and even more importantly, how well they fit in with the prevailing community norms.

Before we get too smug about how smug environmentalists can be, consider the humble cookie. Most of the time, I buy cookies because they taste good, or because they seem like a good value, or simply out of habit. But there's a special kind of cookie that always gets a special kind of treatment. Every year, Girl Scout Julie shows up on our porch sporting her cookie-peddling uniform. My money and I are soon parted, and in a couple of weeks I am scrambling to find a place to store several brightly colored boxes of oddly named cookies. (There is one unplanned benefit of Girl Scout cookies; without them it's unlikely that I would ever clean out the freezer.)

Not only does Julie get me to say yes to the cookies, she does it with a vengeance. She presents me with a list of the names of my neighbors who have also been victims of the Great Cookie Shakedown, along with the precise number of boxes of cookies they've each agreed to buy. I find myself scanning the list for Ed (the fellow a few doors down who always has a nicer yard) and note that he's down for six boxes. I up the ante and proudly announce to Julie my decision to buy seven boxes. That will show Ed, for sure.

The result of this one-two punch of guilt and one-upmanship is an enormous windfall for the young ladies in green: the 2011 annual report for Girl Scouts USA shows revenue of $760 million from cookies alone. Perhaps not surprisingly, Girl Scouts USA engaged IBM to "develop new technologies to modernize the Girl Scout Cookie Program." The first phase of this effort, called the eCookie Project, is designed to "establish baseline requirements for a future product management system" including the ability to accept credit cards in lieu of cash and the development of smartphone applications. They're obviously serious about Thin-Minting a fortune.

So why do I buy Girl Scout Cookies? One simple reason: *because I am supposed to*. It's the social norm; it's what's expected of us from those around us. And that is one heck of a business model.

Our prehistoric brains are wired to keep close tabs on all types of social norms, but there's a specific type that runs especially deep in humans: fairness. A simple thought problem illustrates the power of this wiring.

Imagine that in front of us is a special deck of cards. On one side of each card is a number; on the other side of the card is a symbol. Suppose I tell you that the cards are printed according to a special rule: if the number on one side of a card is even, then the symbol on the other side must be an X. I shuffle the cards and throw four of them on the table. They fall as follows:

| CARD I | CARD 2 | CARD 3 | CARD 4 |
|:------:|:------:|:------:|:------:|
| 8 | 3 | ◆ | X |

Now the question: Which card(s) do you have to turn over to determine whether the "if the number is even, the symbol must be an X" rule has been broken? That is, what's the minimum number of cards you have to turn over, and which ones are they?

The answer is two, and I'm not going to tell you which ones they are (yet).

Now I want you to imagine a slightly different situation. Suppose that you're the parent of four teenage boys. Being the good parent that you are, you have rules, one of which is that if a son borrows the family car, he must fill up the tank with gas. You decide to vacation for a week (who would blame you?), and I agree to watch the kids while you're gone.

Upon your return, you ask whether your sons obeyed the family rule. Perhaps not surprisingly, I reply that I have no clue. However, our mutual friend Pam shows up just in the nick of time. She tells us she's been keeping track of this issue, using one card for each son. On one side she's noted whether the son borrowed the car, and on the other side whether he subsequently filled it up. She tosses the cards on the kitchen table, and they arrange themselves as follows:

| TIM | TOM | TODD | TED |
|-----|-----|------|-----|
| Borrowed the car | Didn't borrow the car | Didn't fill the tank | Filled the tank |

Now, which cards do you need to turn over to see whether any of your good-for-nothing kids broke your family rule about filling up the car if they used it? That is, what's the minimum number of cards you have to turn over, and which ones are they?

Okay, time for the answers to each of these puzzles. In the case of the even/odd deck, you only need to turn over Card 1 and Card 3. Card 1 has an even number, so if there's anything other than an X on the other side, it breaks the rule. Card 3 has something other than an X on it, so if we turn that one over and find an even number, that violates the rule as well. Neither Card 2 nor Card 4 can offer evidence that the rule has been broken; Card 2 has an odd number (so the rule doesn't apply), and Card 4 has an X, which can't violate the rule.

For the car-driving problem, only Tim and Todd could have broken the family rule. Tim borrowed the car, so if he didn't fill it up then he's broken the rule; you should flip over his card to see whether that's the case. Todd didn't fill up the car, so you want to flip his card over to see whether he drove the car (which would be a violation of the rule). Tom didn't borrow the car, so the rule doesn't apply to him; Ted filled the tank, so he couldn't have broken the rule, regardless of whether or not he borrowed the car.

These two problems are absolutely identical in terms of their underlying logic. However, people generally have a much more difficult time solving the first problem than they do the second: about 25 percent get the right answer to problems like the first one, while about 75 percent get the second kind of problem right. In other words, our ability to solve this problem correctly has very little to do with how good we are at logic, and much more to do with how good we are at solving a more practical problem from our past: detecting potential cheaters.

For humans, cheating poses an enormous threat, and this threat was especially significant in the challenging environment that's marked most of our life as a species. Humans are extraordinarily groupish and cooperative. (Some species outdo us in terms of cooperation—ants, termites, bees, and the like—but individuals in those societies are very closely related genetically. They are literally one big family.) Human cooperation is remarkable because it happens easily and frequently even with those to whom we are unrelated. Our cooperative nature offers tremendous advantages to the species by enabling division of labor toward a common goal, specialization, and other benefits. This is great stuff, and in no small part is the secret of our success as a species. By working together—even with people to whom we are unrelated—we all have a bigger pie to share.

But for all of this kumbaya lovefest to work, that bigger pie needs to be divided fairly, and successful, sustainable pie-splitting tends to go south when the cheaters arrive. You know the type; just like Jack, they are nowhere to be found when it's time to pay the dinner bill, tip the waiter, or fetch the car in the rain. Today this sort of selfish behavior is annoying, but in the early days of our species it was a matter of life and death. Thus, to protect the benefits of cooperation, humans became exquisitely tuned to violations of social contracts, to people who might be cutting corners for their advantage and at our expense.

Now back to those two logic puzzles. In the odd-even deck example, the problem is one of logic and logic alone; there's no social contract involved and thus no potential cheating to detect. The cheat-detection circuits wired into our brains fall silent, leaving us with a sterile logic problem to solve. But in the example of filling the family car, there *is indeed* a possibility for breaking a social contract, and somehow our brains know it: Tim and Todd are potential cheaters, and because we're so good at detecting potential violations of social contracts, they stick out like sore thumbs.

In other words, getting the second logic puzzle right is simply a by-product of something quite different and much more practical in the environment in which our brains evolved: protecting ourselves against potential cheating. It's this specific ability, rather than the more general ability to do logic problems, that allows us to solve the family-car problem rather easily but to struggle with the card deck problem.

## SHORTCUT #2: AVOID LOSSES

Imagine that you are the director of the National Center for Immunization and Respiratory Diseases at the Centers for Disease Control and Prevention (CDC) in Atlanta. For the past week, you and your staff have been working hard to figure out how best to tackle an imminent outbreak of an unusual flu strain. You've directed your best epidemiologists to estimate the size of the problem and to propose the best options for dealing with the threat. In your morning "critical situation" meeting, your team offers the following assessment and recommendations:

I. Left unaddressed, the outbreak is expected to result in the deaths of 600 people.

II. The most promising options have been narrowed down to two programs, each of which is identical in terms of cost and ability to execute.

A. If Program A is adopted, 200 people will be saved for sure.

B. If Program B is adopted, there is a 1/3 chance 600 people will be saved, and a 2/3 chance of saving no one.

You discuss the situation with your staff, and as difficult as the choice is, you've made it: you will recommend Program A. You tell your chief of staff to quickly prepare a memo outlining the situation and the two options. He nods, saying that he will clean up the assessment, knowing that you intend to brief the CDC director right away.

Within an hour, you are sitting in the director's office. You explain the situation just as it was reported to you: unless the CDC acts, the nation can expect to lose 600 people. As you hand your boss a written overview, you note that your team has considered two alternatives and that you recommended the first of them. Your boss appears puzzled, noting aloud that she'd have leaned toward the second option. You look carefully at the pre-pared memo and are a bit confused yourself. It notes:

- If Program A is adopted, 400 people will die for sure.
- If Program B is adopted, there is a 1/3 chance that nobody will die, and a 2/3 chance that 600 people will die.

An hour ago, you were pretty clear that the first option was better, but now you're not so sure yourself—the second option does look a bit more attractive. What happened?

Well, your chief of staff inadvertently reframed the two programs (see exhibit 2–1). In your original conversation, the outcomes of both programs were expressed as gains: the 600 deaths were taken as a given, and then each program was described by how many lives would be saved from that baseline. In the memo for your boss, however, the outcomes were described as losses relative to the status quo.

Mathematically, of course, this shouldn't make a difference. Under both versions of Program A, it's certain that 200 people will be saved (and thus 400 people will die). Under both versions of Program B, there's a 1/3 chance that all 600 people will be saved (and thus no one will die), and a 2/3 chance that no one will be saved (and thus all 600 people will die). In other words, the two versions of Program A are mathematically equivalent, as

| Original Description of Two Programs | |
|---|---|
| Program A | 200 people will be saved |
| Program B | 1/3 chance 600 people will be saved<br>2/3 chance no one will be saved |

| Chief of Staff's Description of Two Programs | |
|---|---|
| Program A | 400 people will die |
| Program B | 1/3 chance no one will die<br>2/3 chance 600 people will die |

EXHIBIT 2-1. Different ways of describing the same two (hypothetical) public health programs designed to cope with a deadly outbreak.

| Outcomes Framed as Gains (original version) | | |
|---|---|---|
| Program A | 200 people will be saved | 72% |
| Program B | 1/3 chance that 600 people will be saved<br>2/3 chance that no one will be saved | 28% |

| Outcomes Framed as Losses (chief of staff's version) | | |
|---|---|---|
| Program A | 400 people will die | 22% |
| Program B | 1/3 chance that no one will die<br>2/3 chance that 600 people will die | 78% |

EXHIBIT 2-2. Preferences for different options for a hypothetical public health program. In the top panel, Programs A and B describe outcomes as gains relative to a baseline loss of 600 lives. In the bottom panel, Programs A and B describe those same outcomes as losses relative to status quo. Percentages in the right column indicate subjects' preferences for each program under each framing condition.

are the two versions of Program B. Whether the focus is on the gains or the losses shouldn't matter.

But that's not what happens in practice. Instead, how the choices are framed makes a world of difference in what people choose. As shown in exhibit 2–2, when subjects were presented the scenarios described above, preferences shifted significantly depending on whether outcomes were framed as gains or losses.

People are reliably *averse to losses*. That is, most of us tend to work harder to avoid losses than to pursue gains.

What counts as a loss is usually some type of step away (in the wrong direction) from the status quo. But we also feel loss when we fall short of expectations or of some better outcome we can easily imagine having attained. This is an important point: a loss is always defined relative to a reference point, and the reference point could be the status quo, an expected outcome, or even one that seems like it could have been yours had things just gone a slightly different way.

A good example of falling short of expectations is found in the game of golf. One of the odd aspects of that sport is that holes are assigned par values (i.e., the expected number of strokes to complete the hole for a scratch golfer), but players advance (and win) based on the total number of strokes over an entire round. At the end of the day, it doesn't matter whether you make par on every hole or go over par by one stroke on half the holes and under par by one stroke on the other half. In the end, the only thing that matters is the total number of strokes you took compared to how many your competitors did.

Par shouldn't matter. But in actual performance par *does* matter, apparently because it serves as a powerful indicator of whether a golfer is falling short during the match—more so than even the total number of strokes taken. That is, strokes *over* par feel like losses, and strokes *under* par feel like gains. Because people work harder to avoid losses than they do to pursue gains, golfers should work harder to make par than to stay under par.

And that's exactly what the evidence shows.

In a study of 1.6 million putts of golfers competing on the PGA Tour from 2004 to 2008, researchers at Wharton showed that professional golfers exhibit loss aversion, making putts for par more often than other putts. In other words, when faced with the prospect of going over par, it appears that professional golfers work harder to sink their putts . . . and that as a result, they are more likely to do just that. This effect persists after adjusting for knowledge of the green, the precariousness of the position from which the golfer was putting, differences specific to the tournament in which the golfer was playing, and whether golfers experience additional anxiety or overconfidence when shooting for birdie (i.e., one under par) or par putts. And their extra effort on making par isn't trivial: failing to work this hard on every putt costs professional golfers about $1 million each in annual winnings.

Golfers aren't alone. Loss aversion relative to a salient goal shows up all over the place: baseball players change their behavior as the season is about to end, in an attempt to get their batting average above .300, and high school students are more likely to repeat their SAT exams if they fell just short of a round number.

The human ability to easily imagine alternative states of the world gives loss aversion a lot of room to work, and one of the most interesting areas is regret. That's the realization or belief that a loss could have been avoided had one chosen differently or tried harder.

A clever study peeled back the covers on regret by examining the faces of Olympic medal winners. Using a set of impartial judges, the researchers graded the degree of happiness for each medalist—gold, silver, and bronze. As you'd expect, the gold medalists were pretty darn happy. What's remarkable is that on average, the bronze medalists appeared happier than the silver medalists.

You don't have to compete in the Olympics to feel the loss aversion that gives regret its sting. If you've ever missed a bus or connecting flight by only a few minutes, you know what I am talking about. It's easy to imagine small changes that would have meant making that connection—if you'd only walked a little bit faster, for example—and so it's easy to view the missed connection as a loss. But when you've missed your connection by a lot, it's out of your hands, there's nothing you can do, etc.

We don't really know what's going on in the minds of the Olympians, but it's plausible that what we're seeing on the faces of the silver medalists is regret: these second-place winners could easily imagine having won the gold if they'd only done this or that differently, or just tried a bit harder. Because a different (and better) outcome is so easy to imagine, the silver feels like a loss to them. On the other hand, it's much easier for the third-place bronze medalists to imagine not placing at all than it is to imagine jumping two spots to the gold. Losses loom larger than gains, but what we count as a gain or a loss depends in part on our ability to imagine various alternative states of the world. When the better outcome could have been yours had things gone just a little differently, it's really easy to imagine having achieved the better state. And that can make the current state feel like a loss.

Barely missing your connection hurts like barely missing the gold. Missing your connection by a mile is more like getting the bronze. So next time you miss your connection, remember that you have something in common with Olympic athletes. (Way to go, champ!)

## SHORTCUT #3: GRAB REWARDS NOW, PUSH LOSSES TO THE FUTURE

My wife, Gina, takes exercise very seriously. She walks our dogs a few miles every morning, at a clip that makes me look very dorky when I join in. Back in Atlanta, before we were married, Gina would routinely do a couple of hours of intense yoga daily, so finding a treadmill in her cramped apartment wasn't a surprise. What was a surprise was finding the treadmill at all: it was under a lot of clothes. Even for a fit yogini, there is a tendency for treadmills to become clothes racks.

Gina is in good company. A recent Google search of "treadmill as clothes rack" yields nearly two million hits. "Claire M" of Passaic, New Jersey, is the FourSquare mayor of "my glorified clothes rack (treadmill)." On the Northern Ohio Sports Forum, someone known as "frflashes_vix" posted the following ad:

> For Sale Treadmill —$200 used during one six-week gung-ho push about a year ago—now sits in basement and used to hang clothes on or as a "see what I can do" hazard for my kids and their friends. Excellent condition. Don't know the original price, was given to me as a birthday present from my husband. Let me know if your [*sic*] interested.

The ad doesn't mention whether this couple is still together, but I must admit a certain admiration for the husband's nerve in his selection of birthday gifts.

*Consumer Reports* surveyed owners of home workout gear and found that about a third of them admitted to using the equipment less frequently than they planned. A study in the *Annals of Behavioral Medicine* reported that access to fitness equipment at home increased the initiation of an exercise program but not maintenance of the workout regimen (and might even increase dropout rates).

Why do we earnestly plan on doing the right thing each time we make a New Year's resolution, buy a piece of fitness equipment, or start a weight management routine but far too often wind up back where we started? Doesn't all this mean that we're just fooling ourselves, and that we'd all save a lot of time and money if we'd just be a bit more honest about our lack of interest in behaving better? Not so fast.

### Keeping Track of Now Versus Later

One profession that works hard at keeping track of the value of stuff over time is banking. When a bank makes a loan, it books a cost in the here and now, and obtains a promise of a series of payments over time in return. The sum of those payments is greater than the amount of the loan the bank makes, and the difference reflects the interest charged.

Charging interest for money lent has a long history of being a moral no-no. The early Greeks and Romans were strongly against it. Plato and Aristotle deemed it contrary to the nature of things; Cato, Seneca, and Plutarch likened it to murder. Until the Renaissance, the Catholic Church outlawed clerics from engaging in the practice. At some point, however, clearer heads prevailed, and what was considered bad behavior was charging excessively high interest rather than charging interest per se.

In the sixteenth century, Martín de Azpilcueta and other scholars at the University of Salamanca helped usher in this shift in perspective. Those economists argued that there is a *time value* associated with money. My $100 today is worth more than $100 a year from today, because 1) I know I have the $100 in hand today, and if I lend it out the borrower might default between now and next year; and 2) I could use the $100 in some other fruitful way between now and a year hence.

Most of us feel that $100 today is better than $100 a year from now, and the discount rate is a mathematical means to quantify this difference in value that occurs due to timing. For example, if your discount rate is 5 percent, you should be indifferent between $100 today and $105 one year from today.

The ability to quantitatively handle the time value of money is really handy. Once you have a discount rate, a pot of money today, a pot of money in the future, or even changing streams of revenues and costs over time—all of these can be converted to a single number in the present, which is called the *net present value*. And although there's no right or wrong value for the discount rate, the US government suggests using a rate between 3 percent and 7 percent, with lower rates allowed when evaluating programs that have long time frames (e.g., those that will benefit future generations).

It makes sense that things may be more or less attractive depending on when they happen, and how we feel about time. The government says its discount rate is between 3 percent and 7 percent; very profitable companies might have much higher discount rates (due to the high opportunity cost). But what no one ever uses is a discount rate in the neighborhood of 50 percent. Except, that is, normal people every day.

Consider two alternatives:

Option 1: $100 today
Option 2: $105 a week from today

Which do you prefer? Now consider two more alternatives:

Option A: $100 one year from now
Option B: $105 one year and one week from now

Some people choose Option 1 over Option 2—and that's not a problem. You might have a very good reason for wanting the money sooner rather than later. Some people also choose Option

B over Option A—that's not a problem either; after all, why not wait a week and make $5? The challenge is raised when people do both—that is, choose Option 1 over Option 2, *and* Option B over Option A. It's a problem because no single discount rate explains that pair of selections. Choosing Option 1 over Option 2 requires a weekly discount rate of at least 5 percent, but choosing Option B over Option A implies a weekly discount rate of less than 5 percent.

Most people behave as if they have higher discount rates in the near term and lower discount rates in the future. Behavioral economists and psychologists call this *hyperbolic discounting*. People who hyperbolically discount are impatient for gains in the present but much more patient for gains in the future. Although there is a formal mathematical definition of hyperbolic discounting, a decent rule of thumb is that people give a 50 percent discount to something that occurs later rather than immediately but behave much more patiently when considering delays in the future. In other words, waiting a week isn't a big deal—unless you're asking me to wait right now.

### The Simple Math of Procrastination

Exercise is one of those things in which the effort happens in the here and now, and the payoffs come later. Because of that—costs today for gains in the future—exercise is ripe for procrastination. Here's a simple way to use that 50 percent rule of thumb to think about why that's the case.

Let's say that each workout you do involves 6 units of effort—that's the "cost" of exercising. But you get a future benefit—feel better, live longer, fit into your jeans. Let's say that's worth 10 units. Exhibit 2–3 shows how the math plays out. Because the

| NEW YEAR'S RESOLUTION | | WORKOUT DAY | |
|---|---|---|---|
| 10 units of benefit later | 10 x 50% = 5 | 10 units of benefit later | 10 x 50% = 5 |
| 6 units of effort later | - 6 x 50% = - 3 | 6 units of effort today | - 6 |
| Total | + 2 | Total | - 1 |
| DECISION: I WILL EXERCISE | | DECISION: JUST NOT TODAY | |

EXHIBIT 2-3. The mathematics of procrastination. Future benefits and costs are discounted by 50%; present events are not discounted. This leads to earnest planning about engaging in good behaviors, but difficulty following through with those plans.

benefits of exercise are in the future (relative to when the exercise occurs), they are discounted 50 percent. When you're planning on engaging in exercise, the effort of exercise is also in the future, so it's also discounted 50 percent, and that puts costs and benefits on an even playing field. When it's time to exercise, however, the costs occur in the present (and thus are not discounted), but the benefits remain in the future (and thus are discounted). This steep discounting leads to earnest planning, difficulty following through, and more earnest planning—in other words, cycles of procrastination.

Heavily weighting things in the present has three effects. First, we will tend to bring rewards as close to the present as possible because they will have the greatest psychological payoff. Second, we will push losses, discomfort, and costs as far into the future as possible because their sting will be heavily discounted. Of course, today's future is tomorrow's present; eventually those losses will be felt with full force. Finally, as we just saw, actions that lead to future benefits but have up-front costs will seem attractive when we plan to engage in them, but less attractive when it comes time to implement them.

A strong focus on the present with less regard for the future should seem familiar to parents. It's just what you'd expect if your two-year-old was in charge of immediate decisions and you were in charge of what your family would do next year. Noninvasive studies of the brain suggest this is surprisingly close to what's going on between our ears. One study, for example, found that when presented with an option that includes an immediate outcome (e.g., eat ice cream now), the limbic system lights up. The limbic system is an area of the brain that has been around for a very long time; it's deep inside your brain and includes your pleasure center. When we're considering future outcomes, this system seems to be dead quiet. On the other hand, the prefrontal area of your brain—that's the new, shiny part—seems to respond equally to both present and future outcomes (e.g., eat ice cream now, eat ice cream later).

These findings suggest that when considering activities with outcomes that occur both immediately and in the future (e.g., working out today for future benefits), the two systems are arguing. The prefrontal area is calmly weighing the costs versus the gains regardless of the timing ("the health benefits of working out are greater than the effort working out requires"), while the limbic system is only attending to the things that will happen in the present and ignoring the future benefits ("I don't want to work out—it takes effort!"). When considering outcomes that only happen in the future, however, the limbic system loses interest. That leaves the prefrontal system to make its case calmly, in relative peace and quiet. This is why our plans are generally in line with our long-term interests, and why following through on those well-considered plans is so very difficult.

## THE SEVEN STRATEGIES FOR FIFTY BITS DESIGN

The main hypothesis of *The Power of Fifty Bits* is that people are wired for inattention and inertia. As we've just seen, our brains—and thus our natural inclinations and many of our behaviors—were built for a different time and place. Because we can't pay attention to everything all the time, nature has equipped us with a handful of shortcuts. These are shortcuts that allowed our ancestors to navigate a dangerous environment effectively.

Unfortunately, that environment has changed more quickly than the wiring of our brains. The shortcuts that worked so well long ago on the African savanna are routinely failing us, as evidenced by the persistent gap between our good intentions and the behaviors in which we actually engage.

Just as nearsighted people benefit from lenses that correct the faulty optics of their vision, we will benefit from a set of specific strategies that bridge the gap between the good intentions that we already have and our day-to-day choices and behaviors. Because applying such principles is a deliberate reengineering to address the fundamental processing limitation of our conscious minds, we call it *fifty bits design*.

The next seven chapters present the seven strategies that are at the core of fifty bits design. As shown in exhibit 2–4, three of the strategies are powerful mechanisms for activating the good intentions that most people already have. We can think of these as the "power" strategies; you should use them if possible because it has been repeatedly demonstrated that they can measurably improve choices and behaviors. In addition to these power strategies are three "enhancing" strategies, as well as one overarching strategy.

   I.  Three "Power" Strategies
      A. Require Choice—mandate that people stop and deliberately choose among options (chapter 3)
      B. Lock In Good Intentions—allow people to make decisions today about choices they will face in the future (chapter 4)
      C. Let It Ride—set the default to the desired option and let people opt out if they wish (chapter 5)
  II.  Three "Enhancing" Strategies
      A. Get in the Flow—go to where people's attention is likely to be naturally (chapter 6)
      B. Reframe the Choices—set the framework that people use to think about and react to options (chapter 7)
      C. Piggyback It—make the desired choice or behavior a side effect of something that is already attractive or engaging (chapter 8)
 III.  One Über Strategy
      A. Simplify . . . Wisely—make the right choices frictionless and easy, but create hesitation when a suboptimal choice is likely (chapter 9). I use the term *über* for the final strategy of making some things easy and others hard because in many ways it's the overarching idea for all the strategies: put people on the path to better choices and make that as easy as possible, and slow them down to consciously choose if they're headed in the wrong direction.

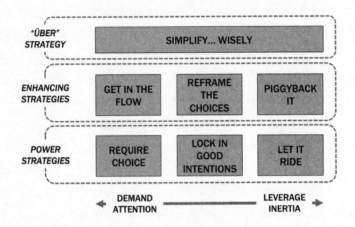

EXHIBIT 2-4. Schematic of the seven strategies. Each strategy is designed to address a specific aspect of the fifty bits challenges of inattention and inertia. The horizontal axis shows which of the two challenges the strategy addresses (inattention versus inertia); the vertical axis categorizes the strategies into three groups (power, enhancing, or über).

Although the order of the chapters isn't critical, I've laid out the book to first address the three power strategies (chapters 3 through 5), then tackle the enhancing strategies (chapters 6 through 8), and close with the über strategy (chapter 9).

Each chapter includes easily recognizable examples of how each strategy has been successfully applied. As you'll see, accomplished fifty bits designers often apply more than one strategy when addressing a behavioral challenge; some of these examples will illustrate that type of approach, keeping the focus on the main strategy being presented in the chapter. Each chapter then closes with some practical considerations that should be kept in mind when implementing the strategy.

# CHAPTER 3

# Require Choice

By the time the Democratic presidential primary process had reached Indiana in early May 2008, nominees Barack Obama and Hillary Clinton had been duking it out for four months. Obama had the edge in terms of delegates, but the kerfuffle caused by the decisions of Florida and Michigan to ignore the Democratic National Committee and move their primaries up in the cycle meant there was a lot of uncertainty about how those delegates would eventually be handled. Both candidates were several hundred delegates away from the 2,117 required to clinch the party's nomination. Obama went on to win the nomination, but not before losing Indiana to Clinton by less than 1 percent of the vote.

In the general election, Obama's team worked overtime to put Indiana in the blue state column. It was anything but a slam dunk. Indiana had been the most Republican of the rust belt states; four years earlier, Bush whipped Kerry by more than 20 percent of the vote. In fact, things looked so tough that of the seventeen news organizations that made predictions about how Indiana would fall, exactly zero gave the state to Obama.

And that's not surprising. After all, four out of five Hoosiers are white, and whites over the age of thirty—who are more likely to vote—favored McCain over Obama by sixteen percentage points. Obama's campaign machine knew they had a tough hill to climb. How could they convince older, white voters to move away from McCain and vote for their candidate?

They knew that changing those voters' minds was unlikely. Instead, they did something a lot more effective: they simply focused on getting out the vote among the youth of Indiana. Although McCain had the edge among older white voters, that advantage evaporated (and then some) for people eighteen to twenty-nine years of age. Among that group, Obama overran McCain two to one. And the Obama advantage held in that age group regardless of race; white voters aged eighteen to twenty-nine preferred Obama over McCain as well (54 percent to 44 percent). The Obama campaign simply skipped trying to change minds among the voters of Indiana, and instead focused on getting more young people to the polls.

Without stating it as such, Obama's campaign staff was counting on *latent demand* for their candidate among a specific segment of voters. They knew that the overriding preference among young voters was for Obama. The issue wasn't more education or persuasion about which candidate to vote for. Their concern wasn't whether young voters were going to vote for Obama. It was that young voters weren't going to vote at all. If that happened, their underlying preference for Obama would stay dormant—the demand for Obama would remain latent.

Team Obama's "get out the vote" campaign worked . . . but just barely. He went on to win Indiana, but only by a gnat's eyelash. For a more powerful strategy to activate latent demand, we need to turn away from the world of politics and to the world of puppies.

## HOW ONE CHARITY SKATED THROUGH THE RECESSION

The period from 2007 to 2011 was a particularly rough patch for the US economy. Gross domestic product was essentially flat (after shrinking in 2008), the unemployment rate jumped from less than 5 percent to more than 9 percent, and the S&P 500 was only off a bit . . . after shedding nearly half of its value in 2008. Perhaps not surprisingly, charitable donations had declined by 3 percent, from a record high of nearly $310 billion in 2007.

But one not-for-profit organization seemed immune to the slumping economy: PetSmart Charities. In fact, individual contributions to that charity were up a whopping 85 percent during that same period, and of the $43 million in cash contributions PetSmart Charities received during 2012, $41.5 million was from individual donors. We all know that puppies and kittens are about as adorable as you can get, but this sort of growth in the midst of a recession is still a bit surprising.

Not-for-profit PetSmart Charities is closely aligned to the for-profit pet supply retailer PetSmart, Inc. And it's in the checkout lines of those retail stores that we find the clue to PetSmart Charities' success. Smack dab in the middle of the transaction— right between ringing up your total and approving the charge on your credit or debit card—a message pops up on the point-of-sale monitor. It poses a simple question:

"Donate money to help save homeless pets?"

The screen conveniently provides a few suggested donation amounts, as well as a giant red NO THANKS button seemingly positioned so that everyone within glaring distance can observe your decision. Gulp.

This approach is known as *active choice*. When using active choice, people are stopped in the middle of a process and are required to make a choice among two or more alternatives. In the case of PetSmart's charity, that means requiring customers to make a decision about donating to help homeless pets. Rather than trying to convince their customers that donating money for animals is better than not making a donation, their application of active choice simply requires people to consciously decide whether or not to donate—thus tapping any latent demand for charitable giving for homeless pets. They understand that their checkout process allows them to grab their customers' fifty bits—to mandate their attention on the question about donating to their charity.

The active choice approach is also frequently applied at the gas pump. Specifically, customers are often asked whether they would like a car wash—no cajoling, no screaming advertisements. Just a halt in the process long enough to tap any latent interest you might have in getting your car a little cleaner. Similarly, many ATMs ask customers during their transaction whether they would like a receipt printed. Businesses are using active choice because it works. They realize that there is a gap between under-lying intentions and everyday behavior, and that one powerful way to close that gap is to simply stop their customers and ask them to make a choice. The more you understand active choice, the more you begin to see its application in everyday life.

## THE PUZZLE OF HOME DELIVERY FOR PRESCRIPTION DRUGS

Patients on maintenance medications—pills they take every day for a chronic condition—have several choices to make. One of those choices is where to get their medications: at a local retail pharmacy or shipped to them from a mail-order pharmacy.

Home delivery of maintenance medications has a lot going for it. Compared to retail pharmacies, home delivery offers better therapy adherence, greater use of lower-cost medications, and higher dispensing accuracy. In addition, many patients enjoy the convenience of having their medications delivered directly to their homes and of managing their medication refills online. Finally, most insurance plans design their copayments so that patients save money when they use home delivery instead of retail. Thus, by nearly every objective measure, home delivery of maintenance medications should be flying off the shelves. Yet, unless they are forced to move, most members use retail instead of home delivery.

There are two ways to interpret this situation. The first goes along the lines of "Objectively, home delivery seems great, but people are voting with their feet—and they're voting for retail pharmacies." Those who choose this interpretation could conclude that home delivery just isn't attractive enough to patients, and as a result might decide to reduce copayments for home delivery even further—a move that could cost employers and insurers dearly—or even to throw in the towel on increasing the use of home delivery entirely.

The second interpretation is completely different, and it's something we learned from Harvard behavioral economist David Laibson. It goes along the lines of "Not so fast. It's possible that people are staying in retail pharmacies not because they like it better than home delivery but because they just haven't gotten around to making the switch." The implication here is that it won't do much good to sweeten the value proposition for home delivery; instead, we need to focus on activating the underlying interest in it. My Express Scripts team was intrigued with this alternative explanation and began to investigate it further.

One way to see which interpretation is correct is to implement active choice: stop patients in their tracks and require that they tell you specifically what they want. If the first explanation is correct, then everyone getting their medications in retail should tell you that retail is precisely where they want to be. But if the second interpretation is correct, a significant fraction of patients should tell you that they'd really rather be getting their medications via home delivery.

We implemented active choice for one large national employer. We identified all the people who were getting their maintenance medications in retail, grabbed them by the (metaphorical) shoulders, and said, "We need you to tell us whether you want to continue to get your medications in retail or get them via home delivery. Either one is okay with us, and we're not changing the financial incentives, but you have to tell us where you want to get your medications."

When we did this, something remarkable happened. Nearly half of the people getting their maintenance medications in retail pharmacies switched to home delivery. As a result, the fraction of prescriptions filled in home delivery jumped from about 15 percent to more than 30 percent. Perhaps even more importantly, the leader of benefits at this company reported "radio silence" from his membership. We figured out how to reproduce this program at scale and now call it *Select Home Delivery* (or SHD).

To date, Express Scripts has implemented SHD for hundreds of clients, and it really does work. Select Home Delivery proved that we could get members to move to a lower-cost, clinically superior channel, without forcing them to move and with little disruption.

Fifty bits designers understand why Select Home Delivery worked so well. Getting your medications from a retail pharmacy usually isn't catastrophic, and there's nothing really fun about switching to home delivery. So lots of patients don't—inattention and inertia set in, and they simply point their fifty bits somewhere else. As a result, most patients end up getting their maintenance medications in a retail pharmacy. Fifty bits also explains why active choice is so powerful: we told people that we needed their attention just long enough for them to make an explicit choice about where they wanted to get their medications. This approach tapped the hidden interest in home delivery among those using retail. No forcing, no persuading . . . just getting their fifty bits pointed in the right direction long enough to make a decision.

## MANAGING A SWEET TOOTH

We've all seen it: the work colleague with the candy dish handily situated right on the corner of his or her desk. Almost every company has one—or even more—of these candy pushers, and they soon become a favorite stop for other workers midmorning and midafternoon. Although it's a lovely gesture for welcoming visitors, having the dish within arm's reach is more dangerous for the host than you might first think.

Brian Wansink, a professor at Cornell University and author of *Mindless Eating: Why We Eat More than We Think,* has made a career investigating our eating patterns and has come to an interesting conclusion: most of the choices we make around food are automatic rather than deliberate, and are therefore shaped by the environment around us. He found, for example, that although Parisians tend to stop eating when they feel full, Chicagoans tend to stop eating when, well, there's nothing left in sight. He's shown that we overestimate the amount of liquid poured into tall, slender glasses and underestimate it when it's poured into short, wide glasses. But one of his most interesting findings involves that beloved office candy dish.

Wansink suspected that clear candy dishes and those within easy reach lead to more mindless consumption. His hypothesis was that using an opaque bowl or setting it a bit farther away would decrease the amount of candy that the employee would eat. And that's exactly what he and his colleagues found: by switching from a clear dish to one that's opaque, or by moving the dish about six feet from the desk (i.e., far enough away that the employee had to get out of the chair to score a candy), people ate about two fewer chocolates per day. This drop meant that they ate about seventy-seven fewer calories each day, which over a year in the office translates to about five pounds of weight loss.

There are several things going on with this simple switch, but one of the main features is that it changed the act of eating candy from something that could be done without thinking to something that required an active decision. Rather than reaching mindlessly for that tasty chocolate, workers in the study had to stop and deliberately decide whether or not to gobble one up.

This same technique can be used at home to help us and our families make decisions that are more closely aligned with our best intentions when it comes to what we eat. For example, when serving dinner we can leave the salad, vegetables, and water pitcher on the table and within reach, and keep the meat, potatoes, and wine (or beer or soda) on the kitchen counter. This rearrangement of food location uses the active choice principle to help us to stop and deliberately decide whether we really want (and need) that extra serving of mashed potatoes before we have a heap of yummy salad. Although it's not likely to turn you into the next Brad Pitt or Jennifer Lawrence, it's a simple switch that will help you bring your best food intentions to life.

## DESIGNING WITH ACTIVE CHOICE

Let's see how we might use the active choice strategy to improve a specific behavior. To do that, we'll use the example of an automobile manufacturer that wants to help its customers to avoid texting while driving. We'll assume that the cars under consideration have the ability to communicate with the driver's smartphone via Bluetooth and include a mechanism for the driver to respond to queries verbally (e.g., through the voice command system used for making hands-free phone calls).

There are three main steps for bringing active choice to life: interrupting an existing process, presenting the key choices, and executing on the choice that the person makes. The easiest of the steps is usually the second; we generally know what choices are on the table when designing a solution. In this instance, the choice the driver must make is pretty straightforward: whether or not to allow her smartphone to send and receive text messages while driving.

The heavy lifting from the design standpoint is identifying a process to interrupt, and then acting on the decision that's been made. For our example, there is an existing process that every driver goes through when using the car: sitting down and starting it. Therefore, one way to apply active choice in this setting is to stop the process of starting up the car and require the driver to decide whether or not to allow texting.

Note that interrupting the process of starting up a car raises lots of potential concerns (e.g., the mechanism used to capture the driver's decision fails, making the car impossible to start). In the case of this example, we decide to replace the full interruption with a pause, and allow the process to continue if no choice is given in a certain time frame. As a result, we decide to delay starting the car for up to five seconds while we wait for the driver to respond. Should the driver not respond in this time period, the car would start normally.

How do we act on the decision that's been made? If the driver decides to allow texting, we don't need to do anything—other than to decide when to ask her again to make a decision about texting. Let's assume that if the driver decides to allow texting, that decision will apply for the rest of the day, and if she decides to prohibit texting, that decision will apply until she turns off the car.

If the driver decides to turn off texting, things get a little tricky because the car needs to be able to alter how the cell phone operates—namely, disabling outbound texting and turning off audio and visual alerts on the phone for inbound text messages. We could accomplish this either by working with smartphone manufacturers or by building an app that drivers could install on their phones.

As you can see from this example, a number of decisions and considerations need to be made when designing with active choice. A few of them are critical and worth highlighting.

First, the decision maker targeted by active choice must have enough information to make the decision. What counts as "enough" depends on which options you present. For PetSmart Charities, for example, there's a fair amount of ambiguity about how the money will be spent and what animals constitute "homeless pets." Because there is an option to proceed without making a donation, however, further specificity isn't critical; someone who is hesitant to donate without that information can elect not to donate. On the other hand, requiring someone to make a selection from a set of options that doesn't include the status quo creates a problem when the information needed to make a choice is absent. Fifty bits designers should think carefully about the minimum amount of information needed to make the decision for which they are designing, whether it's reasonable to assume that people will possess that information, and how best to provide any additional information they might need. In this particular case, some drivers might need to know whether they are permanently turning off texting when driving the car or for some other period of time.

Second, fifty bits designers should decide at the outset whether to allow people to change their decisions after the fact.

There seem to be two schools of thought in this regard. The first is to provide an exception mechanism by which a person can receive approval to change his or her decision for "valid" reasons (e.g., major change in one's economic situation). This approach has the advantage of being perceived as fair, but it incurs the disadvantages of having to discern which exceptions are genuinely valid and of building processes to support and implement the exceptions. (A variant of this approach is to provide an exception process for anyone who changes his or her mind, for any reason at all.) The second approach is to allow no exceptions. This approach has the advantage of making it much easier for staff to handle requests for changes (because none are allowed) but may be seen as unfair. Selecting the best approach depends on the culture of the organization, the nature of the decisions being considered, the cost of making adjustments to individuals' decisions, the ability to operationalize those changes, and other factors. For our car example, we might decide to take a "no exceptions" stance because the text message blocking only applies until the car is turned off. We would be wise, however, to consider allowing texting to emergency numbers (e.g., police).

To put active choice to work, you'll need an existing process in which the person whose good intentions you're trying to activate engages with you, and over which you have sufficient control to stop the person so that a choice among options is required. PetSmart already had just such a process in place; to complete their purchases, customers had to check out at the register. This requirement provided PetSmart with a (relatively) straightforward platform to implement active choice. Requiring consumers at the gas pump to choose between getting or not getting a car wash is handled in a similar fashion.

Other applications are not as easy, generally because there may not be an existing process over which the designer has full control. For example, an employer might want to increase participation in a weight management program by requiring overweight employees to actively decide about whether or not to participate. To make that happen, there needs to be a process in which overweight employees are identified, in which the active choice could be embedded, and in which the employee simply couldn't terminate the process without making an active choice. (This challenge might be overcome by requiring such a choice within a Health Risk Appraisal, but that raises the question of how to maximize engagement in such an appraisal.) In our example, we chose to use the process of starting the car.

In addition, you have to be willing to choose interrupting a process over creating a seamless experience. This is a critical point: mandating choice where no mandate currently exists means interrupting an existing process with the person whose good intentions you're trying to activate. This is not just a technical change; it is a cultural one. For example, most user experience designers work hard to develop interactions that make everything easier for the user. Fifty bits designers work hard to make the right things easier and the less desirable a wee bit harder. It's a subtle but important difference.

Finally, fifty bits designers must be able to execute on the active choice made by each person, at the level of the individual. In the case of PetSmart Charities, this means being able to add the donated amount to the consumer's bill, and then to disperse those collections to the charity (which is legally a separate entity). The more seamless the user experience, the more effective active choice is likely to be, but that often means more "heavy lifting" from the perspective of the fifty bits designer.

**Designing for active** choice—stopping people briefly, "grabbing" their fifty bits, and having them tell you what they want—can effectively close the gap between what people want when they stop to think about it and what they do otherwise due to inertia and lack of attention.

In the next chapter, we take a look at how people can help solve their own fifty bits challenges—by making a decision today that will lead to better behaviors in the future.

CHAPTER 4

# Lock In Good Intentions

**B**efore Gina and I married, I was by many measures a typical guy. By that I mean that although I was living by myself, I had three televisions: one in the bedroom, one in the family room, and a small black-and-white (yes, I am that old) unit in the basement office/workout room. The TVs weren't particularly fancy, and I didn't have anything other than basic cable, but this arrangement allowed me to stay entertained while working out, eating dinner alone, falling asleep, or any other time or place in my man pad.

I eventually convinced Gina to move in with me, which was great. She didn't have a lot of stuff, we had similar attitudes about keeping a place clean, and I was madly in love. That's probably why I didn't balk when she demanded that I get rid of the TVs. Every last one of them.

A few years later, Gina passed the entrance exams for her PhD, and we headed to New York for a long weekend to celebrate. I'd lugged along my 1972 Nikon 35 mm camera, and because we were staying at a nice hotel in Times Square, I was itching to get out on the street to shoot some pictures. But Gina was fried, and so she crawled into bed and watched E! Entertainment Television's *True Hollywood Stories*. Nonstop. For four hours.

Now, there's nothing wrong with zoning out on some mindless entertainment from time to time. But what Gina knew about herself was that 1) she didn't want to waste a lot of time watching television, and 2) that's exactly what she would do if there were easy access to a TV in our home. When Gina asked that we get rid of all the televisions, it wasn't because she didn't like watching TV. To the contrary, she enjoyed it far beyond its being a pleasant diversion.

Removing the television sets today to avoid the temptation of watching too much TV in the future is a type of *precommitment*. Precommitment is a decision made in the present that advantages better behavior in the future. Often, this goal is achieved by making an especially tempting option that one would later regret (e.g., watching hours of junk TV) impossible, difficult, or expensive.

Gina isn't the first or only person to use precommitment. This self-control tool shows up in stories ranging from Homer's *Odyssey* to *Sex and the City*. In the *Odyssey*, the hero, Odysseus, knows that the inhabitants of a nearby island sing an irresistible song, one they use to draw sailors to their deaths on rocky shoals. Wise enough to know that he won't be able to resist the Sirens' song, Odysseus instructs his sailors to put beeswax in their ears and to tie him to the mast. This allows Odysseus to have his cake and eat it too; he is able to hear the beautiful sound of the Sirens' song while living to tell the tale.

Similarly, in *Sex and the City*, the relatively levelheaded Miranda battles her own temptation when it comes to dessert. After wandering into the kitchen and having a bite or two of a luscious chocolate cake, she throws the whole thing in the trash. But even this isn't enough to stop her from eating more (yes, she retrieves the cake from the trash bin for another bite), so she douses what's left with dish soap for good measure.

Precommitment isn't just a fictional device. It is said that in 1592, conquistador Hernán Cortés scuttled all but one of his ships as a means to "motivate" his men to join in his conquest of the Aztecs rather than commit mutiny and head back home. In a more contemporary twist, a handful of states in the United States provide programs that allow individuals to voluntarily add their names to "do not gamble" lists—making it possible for people to make a decision in the here and now to ban themselves from gambling in the future.

Even Kim Kardashian is alleged to have taken a page from the *Sex and the City* dieting strategy, by spraying window cleaner on her food after she's had a bite or two. If you've ever tried to stop drinking, smoking, or eating dessert, you're likely to have at one point or another thrown away all your beer, cigarettes, or ice cream to put some distance between yourself and your temptations.

And if "out of sight, out of mouth" isn't enough to keep the temptation for alcohol at bay, there's Antabuse—a drug that patients can choose to take that will make them very ill should they succumb to their temptation to tipple. (Appropriately, Antabuse is sold by Odyssey Pharmaceuticals.)

## PUTTING PRECOMMITMENT TO WORK

In chapter 5, we will see that automatically enrolling employees into company-sponsored 401(k) retirement plans has proven very effective at increasing individual participation rates in those plans. Specifically, defaulting employees into the program and offering them the option to opt out increased participation rates from 35 percent to the 80–90 percent range.

But human resources professionals and academics alike noticed that once enrolled, few employees increased their level of contribution, even though their pay increased. Because many employees don't contribute at the maximum rate, and because adjusting the rate of their contribution requires action, many participants make suboptimal contributions due to inattention and inertia.

To address this issue, Richard Thaler (coauthor of *Nudge*) and his colleague Shlomo Benartzi developed a program called Save More Tomorrow, or SMarT. With SMarT, employees were given the opportunity to precommit to increase 401(k) contributions as they received scheduled pay raises. These increases would continue with each pay raise until the employee's total annual contribution reached a predetermined level.

Thaler and Benartzi tested their program among various employers, and the results are impressive. In their first implementation, the savings rate for participants jumped from 3.5 percent before the start of the program to 13.6 percent by the time of the employee's fourth raise. Among those who decided not to participate, savings rates stayed flat at about 6 percent. In other words, precommitment caused those employees who were dragging their feet on saving for retirement to leapfrog those who'd enrolled in the 401(k) program but failed to update their contributions as their wages increased.

Dan Ariely and Klaus Wertenbroch studied whether allowing students to set their own deadlines improved performance, and their results are fascinating. First, when given the option, 73 percent of students imposed deadlines on themselves, requiring that they turn in papers prior to the last day of class, even though choosing to wait until the last day would have given them the most flexibility and theoretically minimized any penalties for late papers. However, having evenly spaced deadlines imposed on them led to even better grades on their papers. In a second study, Ariely and Wertenbroch showed that self-imposed deadlines led to better performance than not offering the option to precommit but weren't quite as effective as imposing evenly spaced deadlines on all students. The researchers conclude that although students seem to understand that they have a self-control problem, and are willing to precommit to address that problem, they don't necessarily impose an optimal timing scheme for the deadlines they impose on themselves. It's not clear whether more experienced folks do better at choosing how to time their deadlines, but it's important to note that the students in their first study were professionals enrolled in an executive education program.

We gave precommitment a whirl with a walking program aimed at Express Scripts employees. Between the Thanksgiving and winter holidays, we set up two educational sessions on the health benefits of walking. These sessions were aimed at encouraging employees to attend a group walk with our senior leadership, slated for right after the New Year. Each educational session was identical in terms of the material presented, and attendance at the meeting was completely voluntary. In the sessions, a clinician reviewed the health benefits of walking, pointed out the tendency for people to put on a little additional weight around the holidays, and promoted participation in the group walk. At the end of each session, attendees were asked to complete a short form. The form was used to collect each employee's name and identification number and to ask whether the person planned on attending the group walk.

Unbeknownst to the attendees, we altered the form slightly between the two sessions. In the control arm, attendees were simply asked whether they intended to participate in the group walk. In the intervention arm, we asked attendees whether they would "pledge" to participate in the group walk. The pledge involved signing the form and agreeing to receive an appointment for the group walk on their electronic work calendar. There were no other differences between the two sessions.

We measured two outcomes for each of the sessions. The first was the fraction of attendees who indicated that they planned (or pledged) to participate in the group walk session the following January. When we designed the study, we thought that *pledging* to attend was a more significant statement of commitment than merely saying that you *planned* to attend. We therefore expected that the pledge rate in the intervention group would be lower than the rate of people planning on participating in the control group.

We were wrong. Among the controls, 83 percent indicated they planned to participate in the group walk; in the intervention group, 81 percent pledged to participate, a difference that is practically and statistically insignificant.

The real difference arose when it came to the fraction of session attendees who showed up at the group walk. Among those in the control group who indicated an intention to walk, participation was 23 percent. In other words, only one in four of those who said they'd walk actually did. But among those who'd pledged to participate, the rate jumped to 63 percent—two and a half times the rate in the control group.

Because we didn't have separate arms of the study in which session attendees only signed their names, only pledged, or only got an appointment on their calendar, there's no way to know which of these features was the main active ingredient. Nonetheless, we learned two important lessons regarding precommitment:

1. People earnestly intend to follow through on their plans for better behavior. The rates were identical when we asked people whether they planned to participate in the group walk, and when we asked them to pledge to walk, even requiring them to sign their name. This suggests that both groups really intended to show up for the group walk.

2. Precommitment increases the chance that people follow through on those good intentions. The participation rate for the group walk among those precommitting was much higher than among those indicating that they planned to participate.

## STORK REPELLENT

In 1972, country music star Loretta Lynn cut against the genre's grain by recording "The Pill," a straight-up shout-out about how the revolution in contraception was driving tectonic shifts in the relationships between men and women. The singer laments that the bulk of her married life had been devoted to having and raising children, and then makes it perfectly clear that—thanks to the "Pill"—all of that would come to a screeching halt.

You don't have to be a country music fan to know that oral contraceptives made it possible for women to take much greater control of their reproductive outcomes, and as a result, significantly changed their roles at work and at home. In a *Time* magazine article noting the fiftieth anniversary of the FDA's approval of hormonal contraception, executive editor Nancy Gibbs aptly described the Pill as "the means by which women untied their aprons, scooped up their ambitions and marched eagerly into the new age."

It's no wonder that the Pill was revolutionary. When taken exactly as prescribed—that is, every day, at exactly the same time—it's highly effective, with an annual failure rate of only about 1 percent. That means that if a hundred sexually active women used oral contraceptives exactly as they're supposed to, only one would have an unintended pregnancy over a one-year period.

But from the fifty bits perspective, oral contraceptives are far from ideal. Limited attention means that people are likely to forget to take their medications, so unless pill taking becomes part of a habit, daily adherence is difficult to achieve. Because oral contraception (at least in the United States, as of this writing) requires a prescription, procrastinating on getting refills, and new prescriptions when refills run out, also makes full adherence difficult. These challenges aren't trivial: the failure rate for oral contraceptives in real-world use rises to nearly 9 percent per year, and the failure rate for women under twenty-one years of age is nearly double that.

Let's stop for a minute and think about what this means. When used perfectly, the Pill and other "refillable" methods (hormonal patch, ring) have a low failure rate—about 1 percent. But when these methods are used in the real world, the annual failure rates jump way up. So when it comes to these methods, the problem isn't that they don't work. The problem is that they only work when patients use them as prescribed, and our fifty bits limitation makes doing that really tough.

With many prescriptions, there's simply no way around frequent refills and renewals, so the problem of inattention and inertia keeps coming up. With birth control, though, there's another available approach, including options such as intrauterine devices (IUDs) and implantable hormones (implants). These methods are known as *long-acting reversible contraception* (or LARC), and they have annual failure rates—in actual use—of less than 1 percent. In other words, LARC methods work as well in the real world as the Pill works under idealized conditions, and far better than the Pill under typical conditions.

Why are these methods so effective in real-world use? The key is that LARC methods provide a technical workaround to the fifty bits problems of inattention and inertia. As my colleagues and I noted in a 2013 article in *Health Affairs*:

> Long-acting reversible contraception options require a one-time decision, and once inserted are nearly immune to failures due to forgetting and procrastination. In a large, recent study, long-acting reversible contraception methods were nearly 22 times more effective in preventing unintended pregnancy than "refillable" methods (pills, patches, and vaginal rings). Long-acting methods enjoy superior effectiveness precisely because they recognize the engagement challenge that other methods require (e.g., daily compliance with pill taking) and work around that challenge by making contraception happen automatically once the decision has been made.

More than two-thirds of medication nonadherence is due to inattention and inertia. A large fraction of patients either forget to take their medication as prescribed or procrastinate when it's time for their prescription to be refilled or renewed. The lesson that we can take from the field of contraception is that sometimes a technological fix can neutralize the fifty bits problem. LARC methods transform contraception from ongoing behaviors (taking your pill at the right time every day, refilling your prescription on time, and renewing it before you run out of pills on the last refill) to a one-time decision that requires no ongoing change in behavior. That's a powerful kind of precommitment.

## COMMITMENT CONTRACTS

A different and interesting type of precommitment device is the *commitment contract.* Essentially, this is a binding deal that you make with yourself in which you pay a penalty for failing to achieve a predetermined goal by a set point in time. For example, you could make a contract in which you promise to lose one pound a week for the next ten weeks, with a penalty of $50 each time you fail to meet your goal (i.e., ten "rounds," each with a goal of one pound of weight loss and a stake of $50).

There are a number of variations on how this works in practice, including who serves as the referee to determine whether you met your goal, what the penalty will be (e.g., cash versus admission of failure to your friends and others), how the cash for any monetary penalties is held (to ensure that you keep your commitment), whether certain goals (e.g., losing 10 pounds a week) or penalties (e.g., giving up your firstborn) are not allowed, and to whom the penalties are paid.

One website, StickK.com, provides logistical support for all of these considerations. The site offers several prearranged types of contracts (e.g., weight loss, smoking cessation, exercise) and supports variable types of penalties, from alerting your friends that you either failed or succeeded to charging your credit card when you fail. The site also allows individuals to develop their own commitment contract from scratch (e.g., write one draft chapter of a book every two weeks for the next six months). And in a powerful twist on loss aversion, StickK.com allows individuals to have penalties paid to an "anti-charity"—a group to which the individual would never, ever donate otherwise.

It seems to work. Analysis of StickK.com's user data from 2010 through early 2013 shows that success rates rise as the strength of the user's precommitment rises. Specifically, the chance of successfully completing a commitment among users who simply created a contract but didn't name a referee and didn't put money at stake was 41.3 percent. This rate rises slightly to 44.3 percent when the user names a referee but jumps to 82.6 percent when the user puts money at stake.

It also matters to whom the penalty is paid. StickK.com users can elect to have their money directed to a group of relatively noncontroversial charities (e.g., Red Cross, United Way), or they can designate an "anti-charity" that will receive their money should they fail to achieve their self-imposed goal. To operationalize this feature, StickK.com offers pairs of charities that sit on opposite sides of controversial issues (e.g., NRA Foundation versus Educational Fund to Stop Gun Violence). The theory is that a donation to a charity that is opposed to one of your own deeply held beliefs stings more than a donation to a less objectionable charity. Because we work harder to avoid losses than to pursue gains (see chapter 2), people using the anti-charity approach should enjoy greater success meeting their goals. StickK .com's data support the theory: such users have success rates about 5 percent higher than those users who don't.

Commitment contracts are a very direct way to put precommitment into action; they provide a mechanism that allows people to make better future behavior more attractive than less desirable future behaviors. In the case of StickK.com, this mechanism is a charge to the user's credit card for outcomes associated with less desirable behaviors (e.g., failure to lose a target amount of weight by a specified date).

You'll note that we've now sneakily discussed two slightly different approaches to precommitment. One approach alters the cost of *behaviors* (or choices); the other alters the cost of *outcomes*. For example, when Gina and I removed all the televisions from our home, we altered the cost of watching TV. Now if we want to watch a show on television, we have to invite ourselves over to a friend's house or rent a hotel room, or buy a TV (which without a cable subscription doesn't really offer much in the way of entertainment).

StickK.com, in contrast, allows people to change the costs of outcomes of interest to the site's users. Specifically, users at StickK.com can self-impose a penalty (i.e., fee charged to their credit card) if they fail to meet outcomes they set in advance. For example, I could precommit to lose two pounds of weight per week for the next eight weeks and put $100 at stake each week. This approach makes an undesired outcome (failure to lose weight) even more undesirable in the near term (by attaching a

financial penalty to it). But it doesn't directly change the immediate cost or benefits of behaviors. I can eat a burrito if I like, but
I risk having to pay the piper by the end of the week if I don't
offset those extra calories some other way.

My intuition is that behavior-based precommitment strategies are more effective than those based on outcome. When a
behavior (e.g., eating) and an outcome (e.g., weight) happen at
two different points in time, focusing penalties on the outcome
rather than the behavior may not work as well. As noted in chapter 2, people steeply discount things that happen in the future,
so outcome-based penalties—even those we impose on ourselves
via precommitment—may have to be very steep to work. On
the other hand, when the behavior can't be observed and either
limited or penalized, tying penalties to outcome might be better.

But that's just intuition. From the standpoint of solid evidence, it's a bit too early to tell which of these two different
approaches is more effective, and in what settings.

## WHY PRECOMMITMENT WORKS

As we now know, our tendency to overweight the present and
underweight the future makes it natural for us to plan on behaving better, and just as natural to procrastinate when it comes
time to act. Fortunately, many people understand that they
have a problem with self-control. We've been around this block
before: we earnestly plan on behaving better and then flounder
as we try to follow through. Precommitment exploits this self-
awareness and offers a mechanism by which we can more effectively tie ourselves to the mast, eliminating or reshaping those
options that we know will lure us away from the best course for

us over the longer haul. If people were unaware of the need for a solution such as this, few people would use it.

## DESIGNING WITH PRECOMMITMENT

Applying precommitment to a specific behavioral challenge is very much like applying active choice, but with a twist: the decision you're asking people to make is whether or not to make a tempting, suboptimal option in the future costly or impossible. Accordingly, there are three key steps in applying precommitment: identifying a tempting future behavior, allowing people to choose to make that option impossible or less desirable, and executing on the choice that they make.

To illustrate how to bring precommitment to life, we'll use the example of an employer who wants to increase the consumption of healthier meals in its cafeteria. We'll assume that the cafeteria has a payment system that allows employees to swipe their ID badge and have the cost of their meals deducted from their paycheck. We will also assume that certain food items and meals available in the cafeteria have already been identified as healthy.

The first step in applying precommitment is to identify a tempting behavior. In the case of our example, the tempting behavior is to forgo a healthy meal for one that feels good in the present but we're likely to regret in the future (e.g., passing up a piece of fruit for a slice of pie). There's a pretty good test you can use to decide whether the behavior you're considering is a candidate for precommitment: just ask yourself whether people have ever made New Year's resolutions about it. If the answer is yes, it's likely to be suitable. Eating healthier foods passes this test with flying colors.

Next, you need to offer people the choice to make that tempting future behavior impossible or less desirable. It's at this point that you're helping people reshape the decisions they will face in the future. This reshaping can range from making the tempting option just slightly less attractive than it would otherwise be to taking it completely off the table. For our example, we will allow employees to preorder any of the healthy items from the cafeteria. Specifically, every Friday employees can place an order for meals and individual food items available the following week. Because preordering helps with meal planning, the cafeteria can offer a 15 percent discount on these items.

How does this make eating unhealthy foods less attractive? First, the healthier options will be available at a slight discount. But more importantly, should an employee choose to switch to an unhealthy option after placing his order, he won't get a refund. That is, once he has precommitted to a healthy meal, switching to an unhealthy meal will cost him twice: once for the healthy meal and once for the unhealthy meal.

Finally, we need to execute on the choice that people make when they precommit. In the case of our example, we need to be able to gather orders in advance from employees, make them available on the day they indicate, and provide the 15 percent discount. We decide to build a small website that allows employees to enter their employee ID, choose healthy items and the day they will pick up those items, and deduct the discounted cost of those items from their paycheck. Due to logistical considerations, we decide to have employees print out their receipt for each future day's items and present that to the cashier in the cafeteria. More complicated schemes (e.g., cafeteria staff bagging each employee's orders, providing an express checkout line, delivering the items directly to the employee) could be considered as well.

Although applying precommitment may seem straightforward, there are several issues worthy of careful consideration. How you deal with them will certainly affect whether you'll be successful in putting precommitment to work.

First, you must be able to ask people in the present to make a decision regarding how they want to behave in the future, or what future outcome they want to achieve. Physicians caring for women of childbearing age seeking to prevent unintended pregnancies, for instance, must take time to counsel about various contraceptive methods (or assign trained staff to perform the counseling) and make LARC methods available to women who choose to precommit to contraception. Similarly, the employees who attended our educational sessions on the health benefits of walking were asked to complete a form that allowed each individual the opportunity to commit to participate in the future walking activity. Sometimes you will have a natural point in an interaction where precommitment decisions can be captured, but at other times you will need to create this opportunity.

Fifty bits designers implementing precommitment also need to consider how to make the commitment as binding as possible while allowing exceptions when appropriate. In the case of a weight loss commitment contract, for example, there are some changes in circumstance in which it's desirable to allow the user to "escape" from the contract (e.g., the user discovers she's pregnant) and others in which that is not desirable (e.g., the user discovers a half-off coupon for a pepperoni pizza). Striking this balance is challenging, in part because it often takes a fair amount of effort to determine and verify at the individual level whether the exception is warranted. And if you make granting an exception too easy or the cost of pursuing the tempting option too low, precommitment loses its punch. For example, the US Congress—which has a long-standing and impressive track record when it comes to spending beyond its means—attempted to tie itself to the mast via sequestration, a set of spending cuts designed to be so unpalatable to both Democrats and Republicans that they would have to come to consensus on a better plan. Nice try; sequestration didn't lead to any substantive agreements between the two parties. The penalties were too small and the loopholes too big.

Finally, when considering how to best employ precommitment, fifty bits designers should be aware that both active choice and opt-outs can be used to significantly improve the effectiveness of this approach. By active choice, I mean requiring people to consider precommitment during the course of completing a routine process. This approach will significantly increase the fraction of people who will consider precommitting. If people are not required to make a decision about whether or not to precommit, few may get around to doing so, at least in the absence of a focused campaign.

Once a person is facing a decision about whether or not to precommit, the default precommitment option—things such as the desired goal, duration of the contract, and size of the penalty—is likely to have a significant effect. Researchers at Stanford, for example, made commitment contracts available to employees who wanted to increase the amount of exercise in which they engaged. These contracts allowed employees to commit to exercise at any frequency, for any duration, and with any weekly penalty for missing their goal. Participation was completely voluntary.

Participating employees were randomized to default contract durations of eight weeks, twelve weeks, or sixteen weeks. They found that the contract duration that the employees chose was influenced by the default duration used.

**In this chapter,** we've discussed precommitment—making it possible for a person to make a decision at one point in time that makes tempting future options less desirable (or impossible). In the next chapter, we take a look at how to use the natural human tendency to procrastinate as an ally in the effort to improve behavior.

# CHAPTER 5

# Let It Ride

In 2015, seventy people participated in the largest linked kidney swap in history. Half of the patients were in desperate need of a kidney transplant; the rest were friends, family, and others who wanted to help save a life. The procedure involved seventeen hospitals in eleven states, and dozens of surgeons and medical staff. Such a coordinated swap between incompatible donor-and-recipient pairs is called a *domino exchange*.

To appreciate how a domino exchange works, suppose that my friend needs a kidney transplant, and I am willing to give her one of mine, but we're incompatible. Now suppose a couple across town faces a similar predicament: Joe needs a kidney transplant, and his wife, Jill, is willing to donate one of hers, but they also are incompatible. However, if my kidney is compatible with Joe, and Jill's is compatible with my friend, we're in business.

This sort of swapping can be chained over several pairs, constrained only by the logistics of getting kidneys back and forth, and finding a set of pairs in which the set of donors matches the set of recipients. The 2015 domino exchange—which the National Kidney Registry officially refers to as "Chain 357"—is the largest swap to date. But experts estimate that use of larger domino chains could allow for as many as four thousand additional transplants per year in the United States alone, increasing the total number of kidney transplants per year from roughly sixteen thousand to twenty thousand.

That's the good news. The bad news is that demand for kidney transplants far outstrips supply, and that gap is growing. By the end of 2007, there were about seventy-two thousand patients awaiting kidneys, and three-quarters of them have died or will die before receiving a transplant.

The fundamental challenge with transplantation is an inadequate organ supply. That's what's driving the domino exchanges. Most living donors want to donate their kidney to someone they know, and the domino swap meets this desire because even though their partner recipient isn't getting the donor's kidney, the donor is enabling the transplant for their partner to occur.

But there's another viable—and much, much larger—source of kidneys: cadaver donation, using kidneys from the bodies of people who have recently passed away. Retrieving kidneys from cadavers is far easier to implement if the deceased has recorded his or her preferences about the disposition of the organs. Unfortunately, most people pass away with no preference recorded one way or another. In the United States, the absence of a stated preference is not enough for the organs to be made available. Instead, the next of kin typically must make the call, and they have to do it at a time when they may be overwhelmed with grief and loss.

In some countries, however, consent to donate organs is

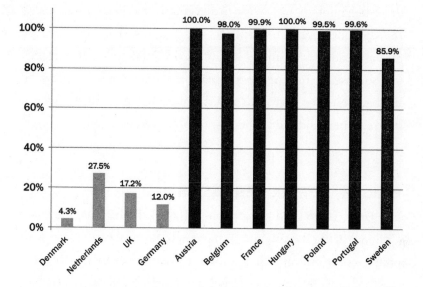

**EXHIBIT 5-1.** Effective consent rates for organ donations by country. The four countries on the left (in gray) require explicit consent (i.e., opt in); the countries on the right (in black) use an opt-out approach instead. Reproduced from E. J. Johnson, & D. Goldstein, (2003). MEDICINE: Do Defaults Save Lives? *Science,* 302(5649), 1338-1339.

presumed unless the deceased had previously stated otherwise. In other words, in some countries kidney donation is opt in; in others, it's opt out. Exhibit 5–1 shows the effective consent rates (i.e., the fraction of suitable donors that are made available for donation) for eleven different European countries. Denmark, the Netherlands, the United Kingdom, and Germany (shown in gray) all require explicit consent; the other seven countries (shown in black) presume consent unless the person opts out. The difference in the effective consent rates between the two groups of countries is striking.

Setting the default to the preferred behavior and allowing people to opt out if they wish is a very powerful mechanism to drive behavior change while preserving individual choice. Using the opt-out approach works so well because it recognizes the human tendency to simply let things ride, and puts that tendency to good use. Instead of procrastination being an obstacle between the bad behavior they're in and the good behavior they prefer, it serves to help individuals lock into preferred behaviors.

## BIGGER, BETTER NEST EGGS

In 1978, Congress added section 401(k) to the Internal Revenue Code, clearing the way for employees to save for retirement with pretax contributions, thus allowing their investments to grow tax-free until retirement. This amendment was a crucial turn of events for both employees and employers. At the time, employers were chafing against defined benefits (i.e., pensions with a defined payout amount), and employees had little say over how the money used to fund their pensions was invested. This new option made it palatable for employers to continue contributing to the future financial well-being of employees while offering employees more direct control over where their retirement savings were invested.

Although the number of employers offering 401(k) plans grew rapidly—by 1983 nearly half of large employers either offered plans or planned to do so—participation in the plans that were offered was less than spectacular. Even with the tax advantages and flexibility of choice, the majority of employees failed to participate in the plans. And the situation didn't really improve much with employee education. One study showed that although most people attending a retirement planning session agreed that they should either start participating in the 401(k) plan or increase the amount of their contribution to that plan, few employees followed through on those intentions.

Even more curious was the modest effect that financial incentives had on employee behavior. Employers were allowed to contribute "matching" funds to employees' 401(k) accounts—essentially free money for those employees who contributed as well. And although increasing match rates increased contributions, the effect was pretty weak.

The whole thing was a disappointing, confusing mess. Employees knew that they should be saving for retirement—and all the statistics showed they were right. But despite tax advantages and the free money offered by employer matching, participation rates remained bogged down in the 30–40 percent range, and perhaps even lower among those who would benefit the most from increased saving.

Into the fray entered David Laibson (the same Laibson from chapter 3) and his colleagues. As noted earlier, Laibson knew about the human inclination to be biased to the present and understood that the resulting cycles of procrastination probably sat at the heart of the problem. After all, participating in a 401(k) plan meant making a series of complicated decisions:

1. Should I participate in the plan?
2. How much should I contribute?
3. How should I allocate my contribution to various asset types, and within types to which specific assets?

None of these decisions is trivial. For example, the decision about how much to contribute implies a change to the employee's paycheck, one that might be easy or not so easy to handle from a cash-flow perspective. Once the employee had worked his or her way through all of that, the decisions would need to be communicated to the company's human resources department, and this meant (gasp!) filling out forms. In short, the benefits of participating in the retirement plan occur in the future, but all of the costs occur in the here and now: the money contributed by the employee, the effort to make the decision, and for heaven's sake the hassle of filling out that paperwork. The road to poor retirement savings was paved with good intentions and littered with unfinished 401(k) enrollment forms.

Laibson knew that this arrangement was a recipe for procrastination. He also knew that there were very straightforward solutions to dealing with that challenge. So he and his team quietly applied everything they knew about how to tame procrastination. In doing so, they contributed in a significant way to solving America's retirement savings problem. With a simple change, Laibson and his partners were able to drive participation rates from the 30–40 percent range up to the neighborhood of 90 percent—without imposing mandatory participation and while preserving individual choice.

The strategy Laibson used was to set the default to the desired option and wait for people to opt out. With this approach, all employees were informed that they would be participating in the 401(k) program at a predetermined contribution rate and asset allocation, unless they requested something different. Specifically, employees who didn't want to participate could opt out by simply letting the human resources department know.

In doing this, Laibson was turning procrastination on its head. Instead of procrastination being the barrier that stands between the status quo and the desired behavior, using an opt-out approach meant that procrastination was standing between the desired behavior and something less desirable.

And it worked like a charm, with 401(k) participation rates jumping from below 40 percent to as high as 90 percent. In addition, employee satisfaction remained exceptionally high, even among those employees who decided not to participate in the plan.

## USING OPT-OUTS FOR PRESCRIPTION MEDICATION USE

As noted in chapter 3, my colleagues and I enjoyed remarkable success when we applied the "require choice" strategy to the decision about where patients got their maintenance medications. Our success with active choice led us to begin thinking seriously about the use of opt-outs to increase participation in the most preferred pharmacy behaviors while preserving choice. During this time, we focused on getting patients to use more generics (lower-cost, equally efficacious medications) and on encouraging those who were getting their medications in retail to do so from the lowest-cost pharmacies. Using an opt-out approach meant provisionally enrolling all eligible patients into our most aggressive programs and giving them between forty-five and sixty days to opt out.

Exhibit 5–2 shows the results of the use of opt-outs, which are quite remarkable. Roughly speaking, making the right choice the default increases the fraction of patients engaging in the desired behavior to as much as 99 percent. And because these shifts occur without forcing patients to make a change (unless they want to change), acceptance of these programs is quite high.

| Preferred Behavior | Success Rate |
|---|---|
| Generic instead of brand-name medication | 93% to 99% |
| Home delivery instead of retail pharmacy | 88% |
| Low-cost instead of other pharmacy | 90% |

EXHIBIT 5-2. Effect of the "opt-out" approach on pharmacy-related behaviors. The success rate reflects the fraction of patients or prescriptions that exhibited the preferred behavior after the approach was implemented. Sources: Nease et al. (Health Affairs 2013), and Express Scripts internal analysis.

## DESIGNING USING OPT-OUTS

To help demonstrate how to put opt-outs to work, let's imagine that we are in charge of a neighborhood homeowners association. As part of that role and in consultation with current homeowners, we have decided on a minimum set of maintenance activities to which all homeowners contribute via annual association fees that are automatically charged to a credit card each owner provides. These routine activities include street maintenance and repairs, landscaping of common areas, periodic collection of leaves in the fall, snowplowing of the private streets in the winter, and the like.

We notice that almost all the homeowners in the association hire help to clean their roof gutters in the spring. Because this activity isn't coordinated, the street sometimes becomes busy with trucks from multiple companies. We've also heard from a handful of homeowners that they forget to clean their gutters.

To address this problem, we decide to bid out the gutter-cleaning business for the entire street. This will allow all of the homeowners who participate to enjoy better pricing and will also reduce traffic. Because we believe that most but not all homeowners would use it, we decide to implement the service as an opt-out program. That is, you will have your gutters cleaned by the chosen service, with the cost being automatically deducted from your credit card, unless you specify in advance that you don't want to participate.

As you can see from the example, there are just a few steps to using the opt-out approach: make the preferred choice the default (i.e., inaction leads to participation in that option), offer the opportunity for people to do something other than the default (i.e., opt out), and then execute on the choices (or lack thereof) that individuals have made.

Although these steps seem straightforward, there's no free lunch, and that's certainly the case if you want to leverage inertia by taking control of the default option. Leveraging the default is exceptionally effective, but it comes with a handful of important practical considerations of which you should be aware prior to giving it a spin.

First, you need to be confident that people have enough information to decide whether opting out is the best choice. Fifty bits designers should be especially thoughtful about providing such information if their opt-out approach doesn't allow people to stick with the status quo. If people can't keep the status quo, the need for information to support their decision about whether to opt out increases.

Second, fifty bits designers should decide at the outset whether to allow people to change their decisions after the fact. As noted in chapter 3, the two main choices are to provide a clear process for exceptions or to make no exceptions at all. Selecting the best approach depends on the nature of the decisions being considered, the cost of making adjustments to individuals' decisions, the ability to operationalize those changes, cultural expectations, and other factors.

Finally, to make the opt-out approach work, you must effectively and efficiently remove those who opt out from the program you've set as the default. This may sound simple, but in practice it nearly always imposes additional effort or costs for the fifty bits designer. For example, to default employees into 401(k) savings plans, the human resources department needs to work with payroll to ensure that only those employees who didn't opt out have contributions withheld from their paychecks. Using opt-outs (as well as requiring choice) by nature creates two or more subgroups of people, each of which needs to be handled differently. This differential handling at the subgroup level nearly always means reprogramming systems and/ or additional ongoing labor.

## IF OPT-OUTS ARE SO GOOD, WHY EVER REQUIRE CHOICE?

Based on our experience and that reported for areas such as personal retirement savings, opt-out is generally more effective than active choice. That said, logistical, legal, and even ethical considerations at times make it impossible for fifty bits designers to automatically assign individuals to a program, which is what's required to implement an opt-out approach. For example, although an opt-out program might generate more donations, charities aren't allowed to take money out of your bank account willy-nilly; you have to actively agree to make the donation.

But suppose you're in one of those situations in which you

are legally able to use an opt-out approach, and that the costs of implementing opt-out and active choice are comparable. You should go ahead with the opt-out approach, right?

Well, not so fast. It's true that an opt-out strategy is likely to be the most effective, at least in terms of increasing the proportion of people that are moving to the preferred option. But if many people are engaged in the nonpreferred option because they really do believe it's the best one for them, implementing an opt-out approach creates a lot of work for them, and for little payoff. From the individual's point of view, the decision between active choice and opt-out boils down to the interplay between three key factors:

1. The effort imposed by requiring everyone to choose among the options if you implement active choice—we'll call this *Effort of AC* for short
2. The effort imposed on those people who decide to opt out if you implement an opt-out approach—we'll call this *Effort of OO* for short
3. The fraction of people for whom the default is not the best option if you implement an opt-out approach—we'll call this *Fraction who would OO* for short

Obviously, as the effort imposed by active choice (#1) goes up, opt-out becomes more attractive. Conversely, as the effort imposed on those people who have to opt out (#2) goes up, active choice becomes more attractive. Similarly, the greater the fraction of people who have to opt out (#3), the more attractive active choice becomes.

When should we use active choice and when should we use opt-out? A good rule of thumb is to compare the relative effort imposed by active choice to that imposed by opt-out to the fraction of people who will opt out. Using the terminology noted above, the relative effort of two approaches is

**Relative Effort of AC to OO = Effort of AC ÷ Effort of OO**

Now we have some guidance for when to use active choice and when to use opt out:

**If Relative Effort of AC to OO *is less than* Fraction who would OO,**
**then use active choice;**
**If Relative Effort of AC to OO *is greater than* Fraction who would OO,**
**then use opt out.**

An example will help clarify how to use this rule of thumb. Let's go back to the case of people taking maintenance medications. Suppose we believe that for most people, receiving those medications through a home delivery pharmacy is better than through a retail pharmacy. Therefore, the design decision is whether to opt everyone into home delivery or to require patients to actively choose between getting their medications through home delivery or retail.

To decide between active choice and opt-out, we need to think about the effort imposed by each approach on those affected, as well as the fraction of people we believe will opt out. As a surrogate for effort, let's use how much time is required to either make a choice or opt out.

Let's assume that we plan to implement active choice using an approach very similar to that used by PetSmart Charities. Specifically, our design envisions that the next time a patient pays for her prescription at a retail pharmacy, a screen pops up asking whether or not she wants to move to home delivery for future prescriptions. The effort required to make a choice is very low: the method of payment has already been entered, the patient is presented with a single screen with very clear options, and all she has to do is click on one button. We estimate that this decision will take fifteen seconds on average. Opting out, on the other hand, requires the patient to call a toll-free number, find and read off her benefits identification number, etc. We estimate that this process will take about five minutes.

Now we can estimate the relative effort of active choice versus opt-out:

$$\text{Relative Effort of AC to OO} = \text{Effort of AC} \div \text{Effort of OO, or}$$
$$\text{Relative Effort of AC to OO} = 15 \text{ seconds} \div 5 \text{ minutes, or}$$
$$\text{Relative Effort of AC to OO} = 5\%$$

So, if we believe that more than 5 percent of people will opt out of the program, then we should use active choice; otherwise we should use opt out. Because 5 percent is a pretty low opt-out rate (i.e., we think more than 5 percent of people will opt out of this program), we decide to implement active choice.

Note that we assumed earlier that the costs of implementing active choice and opt-out were about the same. In reality, that's usually not true; requiring choice generally is more difficult to implement because it requires the designer to handle every single person to which the program applies. With opt-out, the designer only needs to capture the decisions of those folks who decide to opt out. In addition, when you require choice it's important to make sure that the options you offer include the one that is preferred by the individual. Thus, requiring choice usually is more involved than implementing an opt-out approach.

The moral? Use opt-out when it's legally and operationally feasible, as long as opting out isn't too much more trouble than requiring choice, and as long as there won't be a large fraction of people who will be wanting to opt out.

**In this chapter,** we've seen the power of leveraging inertia: if you put people on the path of the desired choice and offer them the opportunity to opt out, the fraction sticking with that option increases dramatically. Using an opt-out approach is the third of the three power strategies. Next, we turn to the first of the three enhancing strategies: if you can't get someone's fifty bits to come to you, go to where you know they will be.

# CHAPTER 6

# Get in the Flow

The next time you make a trip to the grocery store, take a look down the cereal aisle. You'll likely see an overwhelming array of choices. And although the selection is impressive, we all have our favorites. According to the website Ranker.com, here are the top ten favorites (as of this writing):

1. Frosted Flakes—Kellogg's
2. Cap'n Crunch—Quaker Oats
3. Lucky Charms—General Mills
4. Cinnamon Toast Crunch—General Mills
5. Honey Nut Cheerios—General Mills
6. Froot Loops—Kellogg's
7. Cap'n Crunch's Crunch Berries—Quaker Oats
8. Apple Jacks—Kellogg's
9. Fruity Pebbles—Post
10. Rice Krispies—Kellogg's

There are a couple of things you immediately notice from a list like this. One is that there seems to be a lot of sugar "baked in" to our favorite cereals—in both the products and the names. The second is that manufacturers don't seem particularly worried about spelling and punctuation. (Even my favorite Grape-Nuts, which comes in at only forty-fifth, isn't immune to the punctuation issue. I'd never noticed that hyphen.)

But the big lesson here is that the list is dominated by two manufacturers; General Mills and Kellogg's together capture seven of the top ten slots. (Quaker Oats only shows up twice because they managed to create a "son of Cap'n Crunch" through the thoughtful inclusion of *Berries*—which the manufacturer explains are actually "fruit flavored berry shapes.") Breakfast cereal is big business (about $10 billion in annual sales), and over half of that booty is snagged by General Mills and Kellogg's.

What's the secret of their success? Making tasty cereal is undoubtedly part of the equation, but they also break a sweat (and pay, either directly or indirectly) to work with stores to place their products for maximum visibility: roughly at eye height and with lots of "facings." (One facing is a single outward-facing label on the shelf, so a row of four boxes of Frosted Flakes would be four facings.)

Facings and placement make a difference when it comes to packaged goods. A series of studies from INSEAD and Wharton, for example, found that "for the average brand and consumer, doubling the number of facings increased noting by 28%, reexamination by 35%, and choice and consideration by 10%." We can all do the math: a 10 percent increase in how often your product gets chosen in a $10 billion market is nothing to sneeze at.

Kellogg's, General Mills, and nearly every other consumer

packaged goods company knows one thing: if you can't get the attention of consumers, go to where their attention is likely to be. In a grocery store, that means eye level or at an "end cap" (the end of each aisle that we all loop around when we weave our way through the store), with enough of a presence (i.e., facings) so as not to be missed.

In short, if they can't get the fifty bits to point their way, they flip the whole thing around. They go to where they know the fifty bits are likely to be.

## CUES FOR THE CLUELESS, CLUES FOR THE CUE-LESS

You don't have to take over a grocery store to make use of the "get in the flow" strategy. If you've ever left a note on the fridge for a family member (or one for yourself on the bathroom mirror), attached a sticky note to a co-worker's computer monitor, or put a document on her chair, then you've used this fifty bits design strategy. You've put something you want noticed—we'll call it a cue, because it's a call to some type of action—in the natural flow of someone's fifty bits.

Amazon and Netflix both understand the power of getting in the flow of the attention of their users. Both companies mine their enormous stores of behavior data and ratings (for products or movies) to make accurate and specific recommendations for individual customers. They know that your digital screen has your precious fifty bits, and they treat your attention as the scarce resource that it is: they deliver relevant recommendations in which you are likely to be interested. (Think about it: without great analytics, those recommendations would just be spam.)

Express Scripts took the opportunity to get in the flow of patients' attention in a novel way when a few of their dispensing robots in the home delivery pharmacy were equipped with lasers. This technology allows custom messages to be etched onto the caps of the bottles after they are filled with each patient's medicine.

Like a kid with a hammer looking for a nail to whack, we started looking for a problem to solve. It turns out we lost a lot of home delivery customers when they had no more refills left on their prescription. Specifically, among all of the patients who are sent the final refill on their prescription (i.e., who need a new prescription to keep getting their medications), about one-third end up leaving home delivery.

Through the lens of fifty bits, this drift back to retail pharmacies isn't surprising. The patient may not be aware that he's run out of refills and is running low on medication (inattention). Or if he is aware, he may put off calling the doctor's office to get a new prescription (inertia). This means that many patients wait until they are out of medication to get a new prescription. Sometimes the doctor will provide a new prescription over the phone, but other times the patient will need to be seen. When that's the case, there's often a delay due to scheduling the visit. The bottom line is that many patients will experience a gap in medication coverage due to inattention and inertia. By the time they have their new prescription, they may not want to wait to have their medications sent by mail, so they just decide to have it filled at a retail pharmacy.

With this challenge in mind, we decided to etch one of five different messages, or cues, on the bottle caps for patients who were receiving their last refill and therefore needed to renew

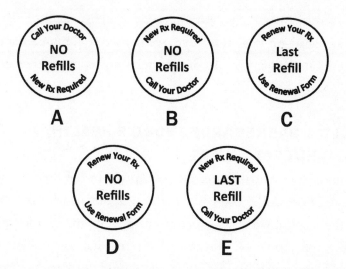

EXHIBIT 6-1. The five prescription renewal messages we tested. The study involved over 300,000 fills, and included a control arm (i.e., no message on the cap).

their prescription (see exhibit 6–1). We tested each of these cues in comparison to a control group—a set of patients who also needed to renew their prescription but got no message on their bottle caps. Patients were assigned to each cue (or the control group) based on the day of the week their bottle was filled (i.e., pretty much randomly).

All of the cues worked better than no message at all, increasing the renewal rate by between 1.5 percent and 2.7 percent. (The winner, by the way, was message A: "Call Your Doctor—NO Refills—New Rx Required.") An increase in the renewal rate of only a few percent may seem trivial, but across our entire patient population it meant that we'd closed hundreds of thousands of gaps in care during the first year alone.

We used the bottle cap as a way to get in the flow of our patients' fifty bits. We knew that it was likely that patients would look at the top of the bottle when they received medications delivered to their home. Although we couldn't tackle procrastination head-on with just a cue, we felt we could put a dent in inattention. And the results of the study showed we were right.

## DIGITAL DASHBOARDS, MOBILE HEALTH, AND A BIG FAT CAVEAT

Automobile dashboards are one way to get in the flow of drivers' attention. All it takes is a slight look down from the view out the windshield, and you can check your speed, fuel tank, water temperature, oil pressure, turn signal status, radio station, and . . . um, never mind; maybe you should just keep your eyes on the road. The British military understood that fighter pilots had a similar problem: lots of relevant information but a profound need to keep their eyes on the view from the cockpit. In the late 1950s, J. M. Naish, a scientist who worked at the Royal Aircraft Establishment in England, developed a system that allowed additional critical information to be projected on the plane's "windscreen"—making it the world's first heads-up display.

Perhaps the most ill-fated digital application of getting in the flow was Google Glass. It's a computer and projection system crammed into a pair of glasses. That means that you can have relevant (and probably irrelevant) data projected right into your line of sight.

But you don't have to wait for the follow-on to these $1,500 glasses to see how technology gets in our flow. A lot of folks—at least in the United States—find their fifty bits pulled with the gravitational force of a black hole toward tiny screens that they cradle in their hands. They're called smartphones—and, increasingly, smartwatches.

The ubiquity of these small screens that seem to get our attention on a regular basis has not escaped the notice of folks in health care. The "mobile health" movement seeks to fully leverage our always-on, highly connected world to help us better manage our medical conditions and to improve our health. Kathleen Sebelius, former director of the Department of Health and Human Services, gushed enthusiastically about the possibilities:

> When we talk about mobile health, we are talking about taking the biggest technology breakthrough of our time and using it to take on one of the greatest national challenges of our time.

Similarly, cardiologist Eric Topol, the chief academic officer at Scripps Health in San Diego, notes, "The smart phone will be the hub of the future of medicine. And it will be your health-medical dashboard."

Here's Topol's view of the brave new world of mobile health, as reported by NBC's Nancy Snyderman:

> Topol speaks of a not-so-distant future where human beings are digitized through sensors in the blood-stream. He explains, "By having a sensor in the blood, we can pick up all sorts of things, whether it's cells coming off an artery lining [indicating heart attack], whether it's the first cancer cell getting in the blood-stream, whether it's the immune system revving up for asthma or diabetes or you name it. All these things will be detected by sensors in the blood which will then talk to the phone."

And when one of these warning signs is picked up by the sensor, a special ring will be sent to your cell phone. Like an engine warning light on your car's dashboard, this ring will indicate that trouble is brewing in a certain area of the body. Ideally, this would prevent life threatening incidents, like heart attack.

Set aside any squeamishness you might be feeling about foreign objects circulating in your bloodstream; guys my age and Topol's certainly remember the 1960s movie *Fantastic Voyage* (in no small part because of the skintight outfit that Raquel Welch sported). The idea may be a bit out there, but only just a bit. Today's smartphones can already be outfitted to serve as EKG monitors, to estimate a person's pulse by capturing minute changes in the color of his face that occur with each heartbeat, to determine optimal corrections for people who need glasses, and to measure blood sugar, blood pressure, sleep quality, and a bunch of other things.

The real question is whether all of this digital magic is going to change anything for the better. There are lots of reasons to question whether early detection of problems is on the whole a good thing. For example, Gil Welch, a physician and researcher at Dartmouth Medical School, and his colleagues argue that we now have the technical ability to detect abnormalities the natural courses of which aren't known. That is, it's now possible to see potential problems so early on that we really have no idea whether they're worth treating. No treatment comes without risk, so this is a genuine issue.

My concern is a bit more mundane than Welch's, but critical for fifty bits designers looking to use the "get in the flow" strategy to advantage better behavior. It's simply this: Topol says that these internal sensors will send a signal to our phones, which will then ring to let us know that there's something wrong. He says it will be like the "check engine" light on the dashboards of our cars.

Hold on to that thought for just a minute. Let's think about the most straightforward of the messages you can get on your car's dashboard: the light that tells you it's time to change your oil. I admit that it's useful; I might simply forget that I've driven the requisite number of miles since my last oil change. But I can also tell you this: if you looked at my actual oil change behavior, you'd see that I am routinely 500 to 1,000 miles late each time. And from that, you'd conclude that I am not that much of a believer in getting my oil changed.

But remember, our built-in inclinations toward inattention and inertia mean that there's often a gap between our underlying intentions and observed behavior. That means that I might actually be convinced of the benefits of oil changes, even if I don't always act that way.

If my laggy approach to oil changes is due to an intent-behavior gap, then why doesn't that oil change light on my dashboard solve the problem? The answer is that the dashboard approach—getting in the flow of the fifty bits—only works if the action we're asking for is rewarding in the here and now, or very, very easy. Remember, a lot of undesirable behavior is driven by inattention *and* inertia. The oil change light addresses the inattention problem, but it does nothing about inertia. There's nothing fun about an oil change, so all of the costs are in the present, and all the benefits are in the future. That's a recipe for procrastination. (I'm not alone in recognizing this problem; a recent Google search for "electrical tape over check engine light" returned over 1.3 million results.)

Now, let's think about what this means when it comes to all those inspiring visions about mobile health. No doubt we will see some amazing technologies that will put health information and even warnings (à la Topol's scenario) before our eyes—via smartphones, digital glasses, Internet-enabled bathroom mirrors, talking refrigerators, and who knows what else. But if these nifty technologies are only reminders, and if the behavior that we're asking people to do isn't either really easy (e.g., pushing a button) or rewarding in the here and now, mobile health won't be solving the whole problem.

## FINDING THE FLOW

When we use the active choice strategy, we take an existing process, insert an interruption, and then require someone to make a specific, deliberate choice before the process resumes. In a very real sense, active choice demands the person's fifty bits long enough to make that decision.

Getting in the flow is a softer flavor of active choice. Instead of interrupting a process to demand someone's fifty bits, we migrate our call to action (i.e., cue) to a setting that is likely to already have someone's attention. Almost any of the five senses can be used as the medium for the cue. Here are some examples of how cues are delivered via different physical senses:

- Vision: Oil change reminder on your car's dashboard, sticky note attached to computer monitor, or note taped to bathroom mirror

- Hearing: Beeper that goes off when the dryer is finished, alarm that goes off when it's time to take your medication, squeaking from brakes when it's time to change the brake pads
- Smell: Odorant added to natural gas to make people aware of dangerous gas leaks

Touch and taste are used far less frequently as media for getting in the flow—which makes them interesting for future applications. The Apple Watch, for example, can be configured to tap the user on the wrist in various ways to signal different notifications.

## DESIGNING BY GETTING IN THE FLOW

Leveraging the "get in the flow" strategy takes just a couple of steps, which we will illustrate with an example taken from the daily life of a young family: a mother of a newborn who wants to periodically remind her husband to pick up disposable diapers on his way to work.

There are just two steps that she needs to take to get in the flow of her husband's precious fifty bits and activate those good intentions. Remember, the idea of getting in the flow is to go where someone's attention is already pointed, so the first step is to find such a place. If your cue (i.e., reminder or call to action) is visual, you want to find a place someone is already looking. If auditory, it will be a place or time someone is already listening. For our example, she decides to use her husband's key ring: he has to pick that up on his way out to the car. (She could also use the dashboard or windshield in his car, but getting to the car keys is easier and just as effective.)

The second step is to insert a cue, making the call to action as easy as possible. In the case of our example, the new mother decides to attach a 3 x 5 card to her husband's key ring, reminding him to pick up the diapers. To make acting on the reminder as easy as possible, she paper-clips a $20 bill to it.

Although getting in the flow is just a two-step process, there are some important features to keep in mind when putting it to work. First, you should make sure what's standing in the way of the desired behavior is forgetfulness. Getting in the flow works the best when you're tackling inattention. If the problem is not inattention but instead is inertia—that is, the desired behavior is effortful in the present but offers a payoff in the future—consider using opt-outs, providing the opportunity for precommitment, or requiring choice. For our example, we will assume that the obstacle to the husband picking up the diapers is that he simply forgets to do it after being asked.

Second, getting in the flow requires that designers find a place to put a cue that gets more than its fair share of someone's attention. This can be a little trickier than you think, often due to changes in technology. Television advertising, for example, counted on the TV as a reliable mechanism for grabbing people's fifty bits because folks would sit on the couch, watching the tube—including commercials. In the early days, keeping the viewer's fifty bits just meant being less unpleasant than getting up off the couch and changing the channel. But with the advent of remote controls and DVRs, those days are over.

The options for where you can put your cue so that it's likely to get in the flow of someone's fifty bits are numerous. You'll undoubtedly be tempted to use the smartphone as your dashboard, because they're displacing older cell phones, most of those folks who have smartphones look at them frequently, and it's relatively inexpensive to create and deliver messages to these devices. The downside is that lots of companies and organizations already know this, so we're all likely to be getting lots of things on our phones trying to grab our fifty bits. The bottom line is that using the smartphone as a means to get in the flow of attention is becoming a well-worn strategy, so many people have figured out ways not to be bothered. If your message is enjoyable or immediately helpful, you have a chance. But if there are lots of other folks trying to squeeze onto the same dashboard you're tackling, be careful—people are a lot less likely to point their fifty bits your way. This means that we need to treat attention like the scarce resource it is.

One of the quickest ways to render this strategy ineffective is to provide a cue that is irrelevant, unnecessary, or not actionable. For example, reminding a driver to change the oil in her car 2,000 miles in advance will probably be ineffective and perhaps even irritating. Ideally, cues should appear when or just before the reminder is actionable. Similarly, cues should be suppressed if the person has already engaged in the desired behavior (e.g., if the driver gets her oil changed just prior to when you'd have otherwise reminded her, the reminder should be skipped). For our example, the new mom only attaches a note when she wants her husband to pick up the diapers, so this isn't an issue.

**Here we have** examined the value of going to where people's fifty bits are likely to be. If we do that, our call to action will get more than its fair share of attention. In the next chapter, we consider how you can reframe available choices to advantage better decisions.

# CHAPTER 7

# Reframe the Choices

Young love is always tricky, but Romeo and Juliet's is trouble from the get-go. The Montagues (his) and the Capulets (hers) are sworn enemies. But nothing is more tempting than something you're not supposed to have, and Romeo and Juliet soon fall deeply in love. When they realize the trouble they're in, Juliet comes up with an incredibly simple fix; Romeo should just change his last name. And if he's not up for that, then she'll change hers. Shakespeare unpacks her logic:

> *O Romeo, Romeo! wherefore art thou Romeo?*
> *Deny thy father and refuse thy name;*
> *Or, if thou wilt not, be but sworn my love,*
> *And I'll no longer be a Capulet. . . .*

> *What's Montague? It is nor hand, nor foot,*
> *Nor arm, nor face, nor any other part*
> *Belonging to a man. O, be some other name!*

*What's in a name? That which we call a rose*
*By any other name would smell as sweet.*

As an engineer, my approach to language was very much in line with Juliet's. That is, I believed that words were just containers for information, "bit buckets" whose only power was convention—everyone agreed what the words meant. A rose by any other name is still a rose. Right?

Well, not so fast. A single set of facts is very often consistent with multiple interpretations, and so it turns out that how those facts are "framed" encourages some interpretations and discourages others. Thus, framing can make a huge difference when it comes to activating the good intentions that most people already have. As a result, some words do a far better job at advancing your cause in the face of that all too rare fifty bits of attention.

To understand the importance of this approach, let's go back for a moment to that screen at PetSmart—the one that I see in the middle of my checkout process (and the one we covered in chapter 3). It poses a simple, unblinking question:

"Donate money to help save homeless pets?"

Ouch. Homeless pets? Sign me up—Junior's tuition can wait.

The phrase *homeless pets* carries a payload of meaning. These aren't *feral cats* or packs of *wild dogs*. They're not even *strays* (which sounds rather temporary, as if Fido made a wrong turn at the fire hydrant). These are *pets*. Pets aren't animals; they are family members. *Pets* belong with people; thus pets belong in homes. And because these are *homeless pets*, we know—in an instant— that something has gone very, very wrong. Their "owners" have died, or fallen on hard times, or no longer love them. Whatever the specifics, each *homeless pet* comes automatically coupled with a terrible story in which a family (or the very idea of family) has been ruptured, and an innocent animal wound up on the business end of this bad turn of events. It's a cold and scary world in which pets are homeless.

Do words matter? Yes, they do. They really do. Consider an alternate plea: donating money for an *animal shelter*. Those words are impersonal (*animal* versus *pet*, *shelter* versus *home*), and the focus of the help is on a building rather than a relationship. But *homeless pets* delivers an enormous emotional punch: notions of family, belongingness, unity, innocence, and either disaster or betrayal are packed into those two words. *Homeless pets*.

## WORDS MATTER—WASHINGTON, DC, EDITION

One of the more polarizing figures in the national political scene is Sarah Palin, the former governor of Alaska, vice presidential running mate of John McCain, and commentator on Fox News. Currently, one of the most divisive subjects is the intersection of the government and health care. Think about it: health care hits all the big nerve endings—health, money, and family. So mixing Palin and health care reform is kind of like playing on a trampoline with nitroglycerine.

But when it came to rallying her supporters on the issue of health care reform, Sarah Palin knocked the cover off the ball—instinctively or accidentally—with her choice of two words: *death panels*. Those two little words—eleven letters and one space—instantly conjure an elite group of stiff, uncaring, slightly constipated bureaucrats whose sole responsibility is to find money to finance health care for a bunch of people you don't know by cutting corners on care for someone you do, most likely your mother. Powerful stuff.

The careful, deliberate use of language to advantage a political position isn't unique to the Republican Party. Consider these examples that bridge both ends of the political spectrum:

> *drilling for oil* versus *exploring for energy*
> *tax cut* versus *tax relief*
> *inheritance tax* versus *death tax*
> *troop escalation* versus *troop surge*
> *universal coverage* versus *Washington takeover*
> *right-wing power grab* versus *voter revolt*
> *conscientious objector* versus *draft dodger*
> *homeless person* versus *bum*

The list goes on and on. Who would argue against *No Child Left Behind*? Who could? And that's the point: imagine talking politics over dinner, this program specifically, and someone raising a hand and announcing, "Wait just a minute! Hold everything! I know a couple of kids who should *definitely* be left behind."

The effectiveness of deliberately framing messages has been proven time and time again. Frames work because, as the politicolinguistic savant Frank Luntz notes, it's not what you say that counts, it's what they hear. And what they hear depends to a large degree on what concepts are activated when we communicate. That's why frames are so important: they provide cues to help us know what to pay attention to and what to ignore, which dimensions of an issue to focus on, what is good and what is bad.

## POSSIBLY THE BEST PUBLIC SERVICE ANNOUNCEMENT . . . EVER

On Earth Day 1971, Keep America Beautiful aired a public service announcement called "The Crying Indian" for the first time. The ad opens with a Native American (played by actor Iron Eyes Cody) in full buckskin, paddling his canoe down a sparkling river to the sound of deep drums. As his paddle dips into the water one more time, we see bits of trash in the river. The music soars threateningly, and the camera pulls back to reveal that the canoe is in a harbor surrounded by smoke-belching factories. The protagonist beaches his canoe on a shoreline strewn with garbage and walks toward a highway. The deep bass voice-over (actor William Conrad) says, "Some people have a deep, abiding respect for the natural beauty that was once this country." A car whizzes by, and an occupant throws what appears to be a bag of leftover fast food out the window; the mess lands on the moccasins of the Native American. "And some people don't," the narrator sneers. "People start pollution. People can stop it." The spot closes as Iron Eyes turns to face the camera, a single tear streaming down his cheek.

This PSA went on to win two Clio Awards and was named by *Ad Age* as one of the top 100 advertising campaigns of the twentieth century. The spot was so darned good that people who weren't even alive when it first aired remember it. And although it's undoubtedly true that there were big cultural forces already in play by the time the spot aired, "The Crying Indian" is indelibly linked to the nascent environmental movement at the time.

Why did the campaign work so well? There's really no way to know what the active ingredients are without a more formal study to isolate them. (Influence guru Bob Cialdini thinks the ad could have been a lot better; he asserts that it falls short because the littered river and shoreline implicitly communicate that littering is common and therefore acceptable.) Taking full advantage of the absence of solid proof, I'll share what I think are two key elements.

First, the ad reframed a very big problem down to human scale. Yes, pollution is bad. But it's also really big, almost too big to appreciate and probably far too big for any one person to make a dent in. Littering, on the other hand, is much more manageable. It's a type of pollution that is within the scale of our daily lives. Littering is to people as pollution is to large organizations. The tagline was about pollution, but the emotional connection was to littering. This is called *telescoping*, and it is a powerful way to connect with people. It's what public radio stations do when they ask us to pledge a dollar a day, stating "that's less than you pay for a cup of coffee."

In addition, the ad reframed what littering means. The ad is telling us that littering isn't just illegal; it's *disrespectful to others*. The ad transmits this frame via a black-braided, buckskin-clad American Indian—the embodiment (at least at that time, in the United States) of a people who were deeply connected with nature. People who litter aren't just making a mess; they're messing with the deeply held values of others. That's a good example of reframing the meaning of an act with a focus on social norms. When it's done well, it can be very powerful.

## TWO MAGIC WORDS IN CUSTOMER SERVICE

When my oldest son landed a full-time job as a customer service agent at a local consumer electronics company, I took him out to dinner to celebrate. Jobs were tight at the time, so finding one that paid a good wage was no small accomplishment.

We ordered, and the server said, "That's great. I will get that right out for you."

Bobby laughed and said, "That's a total customer service line." I asked him what he meant, and he said that the lead of their customer service team had taught all the new agents to periodically add the words *for you* when affirming a customer's request.

Just think about the difference between these two statements:

"I will get that right out."

"I will get that right out *for you*."

Those two little three-letter words tacked on to the end of the sentence do a fair amount of work. They gently move the conversation from one centered on a transaction (you pay for the meal, I bring the food) to one centered more on a social interaction (you're celebrating a new job, I will make it special). I don't know whether folks at Bobby's company formally tested this type of reframing, but I am confident that it helped both the consumer *and* the service agents to make the interaction more personal and less transactional.

## REFRAMING CHOICES USING SOCIAL NORMS

One way to reframe choices is to use social norms. A couple of members of the Express Scripts Consumerology Advisory Board—a select group of some of the nation's leaders in the behavioral sciences—have done some really interesting work in this regard. Noah Goldstein, who is on the faculty at UCLA, is a protégé of persuasion expert Bob Cialdini. He was interested in seeing whether social norms could increase the rate at which hotel guests reused their towels. His research randomized patrons to one of three different signs, each asking guests to consider reusing their towels. The signs differed only in the wording used. The first sign (control group) simply asked guests to "help save the environment" by reusing their towels during their stay. The second sign (social norm) urged the customer to "join your fellow guests in helping to save the environment" and noted that 75 percent of guests participated by using their towels more than once. The third sign (tailored social norm) used the same language as the second sign but tailored the participation statistic to that specific room (e.g., "75 percent of the guests who stayed in this room, #701, participated by using their towels more than once").

Among the control group, 37 percent of guests reused their towels; the rate jumped to 44 percent with social norms, and 49 percent when the social norm was tailored to the specific room. As Noah likes to point out, these results are sort of strange because our behaviors appear to be swayed by strangers who recently slept in the rented bed into which we are about to crawl.

Social norms have also been used to alter energy consumption behaviors in homes. Yale professor Ian Ayres (another Consumerology Advisory Board member) and colleagues evaluated an interesting strategy designed to get people to use less electricity. Building on a small study (in which Goldstein was involved), two utility companies randomized a set of customers to get a report that compared their energy use to that of their neighbors, along with tips to reduce their energy consumption. Energy use was then tracked over time and compared to a control group that didn't receive the social messaging. The researchers found that the social norms approach reduced energy consumption by about 1 percent to 2 percent. This reduction may seem modest—unless you've ever tried to get people to voluntarily cut back on how much energy they use.

Social norms are tricky because what counts as a norm is tightly connected to which group you associate with. John Beshears and colleagues used social norms messaging in an attempt to increase 401(k) participation. They sent communications to employees who weren't taking full advantage of the company's personal retirement savings plan, then evaluated social norms as a means to improve participation. Specifically, the communications shared the participation rates of other employees of a similar age, which ranged from 72 percent to 93 percent. The social norms messaging worked, but only among nonunionized employees. In that group, the social norms message increased participation by about 2 percent. But the social norms message backfired among union employees, whose participation rate *dropped* by more than 3 percent. In fact, the greater the social norms aspect of the message (i.e., the greater the stated fraction of other like-aged employees participating in the plan), the *lower* the participation rate among union employees.

The moral of the story is that if you're trying to use social norms to advantage better behavior, you'd best be careful. By definition, social norms invoke the concept of a group (e.g., your neighbors, people who stayed in the same hotel room, teammates in a sport). If there are people who are in a group, that means there are people who aren't in the group, and those outsiders may react *against* the behavior of the "in group." In fact, a closer look at the positive results of using social norms on energy use revealed a similar pattern. The effect of social norms on politically liberal households was as much as two to four times greater than on politically conservative households but was actually counterproductive (i.e., energy use *increased*) among conservatives who were informed that they were doing better than average.

## REFRAMING CHOICES USING LOSS AVERSION

One of the most important things to keep in mind when using financial incentives to motivate behavior change is loss aversion, one of the three shortcuts we discussed in chapter 2. What about situations in which you're trying to get someone to act in a way that will save him or her money? Use communications that change the decision maker's frame of reference and therefore the light in which he or she sees the desired behavior.

Here's an example from my experience at Express Scripts. We realized that many patients had an opportunity to save money by switching from a more expensive branded medication to an equally effective but lower-cost generic option. Loss aversion suggests that people work harder to avoid losses than they do to pursue gains; framing tells us that words matter. So instead of talking about the money patients could save by making the switch to the lower-cost option, we reframed the communication to emphasize the money they were losing by *not* making the switch. Specifically, we likened using an expensive branded medication when a less expensive option is available to "burning money." The approach worked, nearly doubling the performance of the communication.

There's one more aspect of framing to keep in mind when dealing with financial incentives: bundling versus enumerating. Because losses loom larger than gains, in general it's a good idea to bundle the losses—one big loss is less painful than "death by a thousand cuts." In addition, because gains are often undervalued, it's best to enumerate them.

Amazon Prime is a great example of bundling losses and enumerating gains. Consumers who've signed up for this service pay a one-time, up-front fee for free shipping on most orders over the ensuing year. Instead of inducing losses every time you buy something (by charging a shipping fee), Amazon bundles all of those into a one-time fee. Every time you shop, you can see which items are eligible for Amazon Prime free shipping. And every time you buy something, Amazon reminds you that shipping is free. They bundle the losses and enumerate the gains.

Hopefully, you're getting the idea that reframing goes well beyond spin—euphemistic "newspeak" that whitewashes key issues or problems. Frames are the lenses through which we see the world, and they typically include baked-in assumptions. Because they're rarely neutral, frames make some conclusions easier or more attractive than others. In the rest of this chapter, we will consider these broader aspects of framing, and how fifty bits designers can use framing to activate better decisions.

## FOCUSING ATTENTION ON A KEY ATTRIBUTE

Most interesting choices require trade-offs. Premium ice cream may taste better but cost more; the trade-off in that case is between taste and price. When you show up at the movie theater to see the latest release from your favorite director and discover the show is sold out, you have to decide whether to wait for the next available show or to see something you're not quite as keen on. Sometimes the trade-offs are front and center; other times, not so much. How you present a set of options can communicate quite a bit about how people should handle these trade-offs.

Consider, for example, the curious "decoy" effect. Imagine you're making your first trip to an unfamiliar town. You ask the nice gentleman at the hotel's front desk for a dinner recommendation. He gives you two suggestions: the first is a restaurant with a five-star rating that's a twenty-five-minute ride away; the second has a rating of three stars but is only five minutes away. As you ponder whether the higher-rated restaurant is worth the extra drive, he offers a third option: another five-star restaurant that is thirty-five minutes away. Because the third option is no better than the first, it shouldn't affect your decision.

But it does: it increases the attractiveness of the option that is clearly superior to it, in this case the five-star restaurant that's just a bit closer. If the desk clerk had instead offered an additional option that made the second suggestion look better in relative terms (e.g., a one-star joint also five minutes away), we'd be more likely to choose the closer, lower-rated restaurant. No one's really sure exactly how the decoy effect works, but one explanation is that adding the third option cues our attention toward one of the two attributes that we have to trade off in making the choice.

Using a decoy is just one way to focus attention on one of several attributes. Another effective approach is to present the options in a sorted order. Consider, for example, the menu at a traditional Italian restaurant. The first set of items is the *antipasti*, which you can think of as appetizers. Next come the *primi* (literally, "firsts") which are almost always pasta dishes, followed by *secondi* (you guessed it, "seconds"), which are typically meat or fish dishes. I have no idea how the Italians can eat like this without becoming fat, but most of them seem to manage.

The items on the Italian menu aren't listed by price, but instead subtly indicate how you should organize your meal: appetizers followed by a pasta dish and then a protein. And although not every Italian eats like this all the time, to do so is commonplace. The menu creates a frame—an organizing framework for your meal. Thus, the trade-offs generally happen within the frame: this appetizer *versus* that one, or this pasta dish *versus* another.

The simplest kind of menu is a list of options that is ordered along one dimension. This could be price, some measure of performance, or any other attribute. Once you've ordered the list along that attribute, you can be pretty confident that that dimension will be front and center during the decision-making process. As we'll see in chapter 10, presenting contraceptive options to women starting with the most effective and then working down to the least effective can be part of a powerful method for activating good intentions.

## DESIGNING BY REFRAMING THE CHOICES

To help demonstrate how to apply the strategy of reframing choices, we'll use the example of a human resources professional, Jim, who has the unenviable responsibility of letting employees know that the amount that they need to contribute toward their health insurance is going up next year. Let's see how Jim might best reframe this message to his employees in three major steps.

First, we need to identify a new frame that puts the message in the most effective light. This is sometimes difficult to do, and in the case of our example, there doesn't seem to be any upside at all to increased health insurance costs for the employees. But there is: in the absence of greater financial contributions from employees, the employer would eventually have to drop insurance coverage altogether. In other words, this change is needed if health insurance coverage by the employer is to be preserved.

Next, we need to find a concept that already exists in people's minds that can be used to activate the new frame. For our example, the core idea that we want to activate is preservation of something valuable to the employee. After a fair amount of thinking, we decide to leverage the concept of an endangered list. This concept is a good one because almost everyone has heard of an endangered list, and because that phrase instantly conjures up powerful ideas: things on the endangered list need to be protected, for without that protection they are likely to go extinct.

Finally, we need to develop and deploy a message using that frame. In the case of our example, we need to tie health benefits to the concept of an endangered list. We do this with the simple message "Health costs have risen for years, threatening our ability to provide those benefits in the days ahead. We need to help keep benefits off the endangered list. Increasing your monthly contribution by $20—less than a dollar a day—will help protect your benefits."

A different kind of reframing—and one that borders on sneaky—preserves choice but limits it by offering a narrow set of options. Wise parents understand the power of such an approach. For example, consider a young child who routinely refuses to put on his coat when it's time to go to school in the winter. One approach is the "because I said so" strategy; those of us who are parents appreciate how deflating this method can be for all involved. A different approach reframes the situation by presenting two different options and letting the child choose by asking him, "Would you rather put your coat on now or carry it with you to school for later?"

Reframing the language you use has a relatively small upfront cost, as typically you are only changing words on a page, language in a discussion, copy on a website or in an e-mail, etc. Getting that all right, however, takes investment in two areas. First, you need to hire talented communicators who understand the importance of the words they use. Do your writers understand that people are wired to be especially sensitive to losses, the group, and the present? Do they know that the best communications often involve a turn of phrase that activates concepts that already have high equity in people's minds?

Second, I strongly encourage you to test all of your communications. This is best done in a head-to-head fashion, including the use of a no-message group (i.e., a control group that receives no messaging at all). This approach is valuable because what might seem like a surefire message may have little—or even a negative—effect. Furthermore, writers and marketers sometimes have an unrealistic sense of the effect that communications can have on individual behavior, so looking to the evidence about what's working and how well it's working is critical.

Despite these hurdles, reframing can be a very effective and powerful method for increasing the rate at which people engage in desirable behaviors and make choices that will serve them well over the longer term.

Reframing choices is probably the most difficult of all the seven strategies to apply effectively. Reframing requires a delicate touch; go too far and people will (rightly) see your messaging as an attempt to camouflage bad news or to "put lipstick on a pig." In contrast, well-designed reframing provides a mechanism that allows an alternative and legitimate view of the situation to be appreciated. Also, at its most effective, reframing leverages well-accepted concepts that are already in people's heads. Thus, communicators and writers who are the most effective typically have a very broad repertoire of ideas from which to select.

We now know that people are wired for inattention and inertia. This is what we've been calling the "fifty bits" problem. This chapter has focused on the power of reframing the choices people face to advantage better behaviors and decisions. In the next chapter, we explore an especially interesting strategy: piggybacking the desired behavior on one that we know people enjoy in the here and now.

# CHAPTER 8

# Piggyback It

After writing songs piecemeal for Walt Disney's movies, brothers Bob and Dick Sherman had finally hit the big time. Disney asked them to write all the songs for his upcoming movie *Mary Poppins*. Things progressed nicely, with Julie Andrews eventually agreeing to play the title role. The Sherman brothers had nailed down several songs, including a ballad specifically for Ms. Andrews, entitled "Her Philosophy." As Richard Sherman later recounted, "She didn't like it. She felt it wasn't crisp enough, it wasn't bright enough for the Mary Poppins character. She wanted something that really epitomized her personality."

The brothers struggled to find a replacement song. They agreed that they needed some sort of upbeat hook but couldn't settle on one they both liked. Returning home one afternoon, Bob Sherman asked his young son Jeff about the day's events. According to Richard, a pivotal conversation followed:

And Bob said "Jeff, what did you do today?" and Jeff said, "Well, we had the polio vaccine today." He said, "Did it hurt?" "Oh, no, no, no. They put it on a cube of sugar and they put it in a little plastic spoon and you took it in your mouth, and it was candy. It was delicious." My brother came in the next day with this glassy-eyed expression. He says, "I think I got the title. I think I've got the title."

The next morning they shared an early draft of the new song with Disney, who quickly agreed with the direction. And so the song "A Spoonful of Sugar" was born.

The sixth strategy in the arsenal of the fifty bits designer is *piggybacking*. Rather than tackle the desired behavior head-on, piggybacking makes that behavior the side effect of something that people are already likely to pursue or enjoy. With piggybacking, the behavior we desire "catches a ride" with something that we know that people want to do. In the case of the polio vaccine, receiving a vaccination piggybacks on eating a sugar cube.

## THE POWER OF MINT

Piggybacking is the secret powering one of America's few successes of instilling healthy habits at a population level: tooth brushing. In his exceptional book *The Power of Habit*, journalist Charles Duhigg explains how this change came to pass. Although tooth brushing has been around for thousands of years (Egyptians apparently used twigs and leaves to do it), it didn't really take off until the introduction of Pepsodent—a toothpaste introduced in the early twentieth century. In the decade that followed the introduction of this new product, the prevalence of tooth brushing skyrocketed.

Why the big shift in behavior? Unlike competing formulations, Pepsodent was designed to taste minty and was positioned to remove the "mucin film" that naturally forms on teeth. For the first time, brushing your teeth felt good in the here and now: the slimy film was removed, and your mouth was left cool and tingling from the mint. In other words, prevention of cavities in the future—the real health benefit of daily brushing—is piggybacking on the clean feeling that tooth brushing generates in the here and now.

Using piggybacking to drive better behavior happens in public as well as private bathrooms. As noted in Richard Thaler and Cass Sunstein's *Nudge*, folks who take care of public bathrooms have to deal with what is euphemistically called "overspray" in urinals. At some point, a manager at the Schiphol Airport outside of Amsterdam came up with a solution: he had pictures of flies etched onto the inside of urinals. By carefully positioning the targets, overspray was minimized by a reported 80 percent. Those flies now appear in public urinals around the world, turning careful urination into one of boys' favorite games: aiming their stream.

## ACCIDENTAL EXERCISE

Not too many years ago, Volkswagen sponsored a campaign called "The Fun Theory." Designers identified virtuous behaviors and then created fun interactions that nudged greater engagement in those behaviors. For example, at a subway station riders had the choice between taking the stairs or the escalator; prior to the redesign, many of them took the nearly effortless escalator. Overnight, the designers turned the stairs into a giant, functioning piano keyboard. That is, riders could play tunes by walking up and down the stairs. As a result, more people took the stairs. Similar approaches were used to nudge greater use of trash bins, bottle recycling, and adherence to the speed limit. (You can see videos of these examples and learn more about the initiative at http://www.thefuntheory.com.)

We use piggybacking at our house, too. Although Gina prevailed on her desire to rid our place of televisions, there's one exception. In our unfinished basement, we have a single monitor with access to a low-cost video streaming service (e.g., Netflix, Amazon). The monitor is placed directly in front of our treadmill. Although this arrangement makes it nearly impossible to go down to the basement to relax and zone out watching TV (you have to stand up, on a treadmill, in an unfinished basement), it does exactly what we need it to do: it piggybacks exercise on entertainment. That is, exercising on the treadmill is a natural side effect of watching TV in our house.

## PIGGYBACKING ON A LAUGH: BURMA-SHAVE

In 1925, Clinton Odell introduced a product called Burma-Shave. Burma-Shave was sort of a breakthrough in the technology of shaving, because it was a brushless shaving cream. But its real claim to fame was the unique advertising campaign it employed. Starting in about 1928, Burma-Shave placed small billboards along roadways. First deployed in Minneapolis, the signs spread throughout most of the continental United States. The signs were designed to be read sequentially as people drove along the roads.

At first, the signs were fairly straightforward in terms of their sales pitch, and then later employed humor. Some examples show the evolution of the Burma-Shave message:

1927: Shave the modern way / No brush / No lather / No rub-in / Big tube 35 cents—Drug stores / Burma-Shave

1928: Takes the "H" out of shave / Makes it save / Saves complexion / Saves time and money / No brush—no lather / Burma-Shave

1929: Every shaver / Now can snore / Six more minutes / Than before / By using / Burma-Shave

1930: Does your husband / Misbehave / Grunt and grumble / Rant and rave / Shoot the brute some / Burma-Shave

1935: Keep well / To the right / Of the oncoming car / Get your close shaves / From the half-pound jar / Burma-Shave

At its peak, Burma-Shave was the second-highest-selling brushless shaving cream. Why did these advertisements work so well? First, they employed the "get in the flow" strategy—particularly effective for people on a long drive in the middle of the country. But take another look at the evolution of the Burma-Shave messages: first, the straight sales message, then a shift to humor, and then to humor plus safety messages. At its best, the Burma-Shave pitch piggybacked on a serious message delivered in an entertaining way. It's hard to get any better than that.

Although the Burma-Shave billboards are long gone, the use of humor to change behavior is not. Companies like Jellyvision of Chicago specialize in the development of interactive Web conversations that work in part because engaging in them is inherently enjoyable. We tested such an interactive Web conversation (IWC) to help educate patients about the potential benefits of using our home delivery pharmacy as part of Select Home Delivery (see chapter 3). The IWC used light humor and cartoon-style graphics, with the goal of making learning about home delivery a side effect of being entertained. The results were quite positive: conversion rates jumped from 53 percent to 64 percent.

## WHAT HAPPENS IN VEGAS COULD HAPPEN AT HOME

Here's an instructive approach to helping patients be more adherent to their blood-thinning medications: make pill taking a side effect of playing the lottery. Participants in the study were given a special electronic pillbox for their medications. The pillbox connected via telephone line, making it possible for the researchers to observe whether patients adhered to their medications on a daily basis. Patients in the intervention arm were entered into a lottery each day; the lottery offered a 1-in-5 chance of winning $10 as well as a 1-in-100 chance of winning $100. Winning participants who took their medication that day were rewarded with their winnings; those who won but failed to take their medication were notified that they would not be receiving the winnings (a clever use of loss aversion). Subjects in the control arm used the same device but were not enrolled in the lottery. Subjects in the intervention group showed a trend to better adherence and greater control of INR (a key measurement of the proper blood thinning), although the differences were not statistically significant. The study was relatively small (101 subjects), which might explain the lack of statistical significance.

A similar approach was tested as a means to help people lose weight—specifically, one pound a week for sixteen weeks. In this study, on every day a subject in the intervention group reported a weight that was at or below the target weight for that day, the subject was entered into a lottery. As with the blood-thinner study, the lottery offered a 1-in-5 chance of winning $10 and a 1-in-100 chance of winning $100 and people in the control group only had monthly weigh-ins. Subjects in the lottery arm lost an average of 13.1 pounds, while those in the control group only lost an average of 3.9 pounds. (The lottery was stopped after sixteen weeks, and at seven months the difference between the groups was no longer statistically significant.) Very similar results were found with a longer weight-loss phase followed by an eight-week maintenance phase (i.e., statistically significant weight loss during the intervention with loss of statistical significance over the longer term).

## DESIGNING WITH PIGGYBACKING

To demonstrate how to implement piggybacking, let's use the example of an elementary school teacher who is trying to help his students memorize the US state capitals. Putting piggybacking to work is a two-step process. First, after we've identified the behavior we're trying to promote, we must find a different behavior that most people find fun, entertaining, or pleasant. This naturally desirable behavior is what we will piggyback on. For our example, our teacher notes the great interest most kids in his class seem to have for weekly talent shows like *American Idol* and *The Voice*. He concludes that performing in and watching such shows is a possible vehicle.

Next, we must figure out a way to piggyback the desired behavior onto that vehicle. This is the tricky part of piggybacking. We want to find a way to make the desired behavior a side effect of participating in another behavior that's inherently fun or pleasant. In the case of our example, the teacher splits the class into five teams, assigning each to develop a song. The only requirement for the song is that each capital must be clearly tied to each state. The class will have a talent show competition in three weeks' time to debut their songs, and each member of the team must participate in some way.

Piggybacking is very promising because it's based on using a behavior or activity that's attractive in the here and now. There are a few considerations that are important to keep in mind when using this fifty bits design strategy, however.

First, it often takes a fair degree of creativity and thought to find a behavior on which you can successfully piggyback. Give yourself time to identify a set of potential ways to make the desired behavior a side effect of something else that people already want to do. You may find this to be a bit of a trial-and-error process.

Making piggybacking work also typically involves the need to reengineer one process or another. In the case of exercise in our basement, for example, I had to mount the display in front of the treadmill, run the connection from our DSL modem to the box that streams the media, set up the right audio so I could hear over the noise of the treadmill, etc. The polio vaccine could piggyback on the sugar cube, but only because the vaccine was designed to be taken orally. In the study that piggybacked pill taking on a lottery game, a completely new device had to be provided to the patients; this device allowed the investigators to know whether a patient was "playing" the lottery. In addition, the lottery wasn't free—every day patients took their medication, they had a 1-in-5 chance of winning $10 and a 1-in-100 chance of winning $100. This means that the designers had to pay out an average of $3 per adherent patient per day and arrange for making those payments (issuing a check, keeping track of the payments, 1099 forms, and so on).

Despite these hurdles, piggybacking can be a very effective and powerful strategy for increasing the rate at which people engage in desirable behaviors and make choices that will serve them well over the longer term.

So far, this section has described six strategies that fifty bits designers can use to address the twin challenges of inattention and inertia: requiring choice, locking in good intentions, using opt-outs, getting in the flow of people's attention, reframing the choices, and piggybacking. The last of these strategies serves as a reminder of the power of easy—how making the right behavior as easy as possible often leads to outsized effects. As we'll see, this effect also implies that we may need to make the *wrong* choice a bit harder as well.

# CHAPTER 9

# Simplify Wisely

During the first week of July 2008, US gas prices peaked above $4 per gallon. Americans, addicted to big cars in the driveway and small bills at the pump, lost their tempers, their patience, and no small measure of their pride. The war in Iraq was dragging on, the dollar was off against the euro (as well as against the Albanian lek . . . the lek!), "untouchable" Eliot Spitzer had taken a swan dive from grace and into Room 871 of the Mayflower Hotel (reportedly sporting nothing but midlength black calf socks), Jennifer Aniston had stooped to dating John Mayer, and Barack Obama trailed Jon Stewart by ten points in the polls. That very week America was having a birthday, but it was her party, and she'd cry if she wanted.

The folks taking the brunt of the run-up in gas prices were, of course, those who could afford it the least—those who had been just getting by when gas was only $2 per gallon. They couldn't manage $3, and at $4, well, people began to talk seriously about "peak oil"—the point in time at which global production of oil crests and subsequently enters inextricable decline, resulting in ever-increasing prices. To give a proper sense of just how horrible things had become, consider this: some Americans actually started using public transportation.

And right behind them in terms of brunt-taking was America's youth. Sky-high gas prices meant that instead of kids borrowing their parents' cars for trips down to the mall, parents borrowed their kids' ears for trips down memory lane. Across the country, parents recalled, "When I was your age, gas cost $X$ dollars a gallon," $X$ being a number that decreased monotonically with their parents' age. These fogies believed they were connecting their children to the past, as had their parents before them; kids believed their parents were living in the past, as had their parents before them, too. The circle of life—but in this case more like a rotary engine and no gas in the tank.

The pain of high fuel cost spread beyond pimply-faced teens wanting to get from here to as far away from here as possible. But if there's one thing Americans know how to do, it's how to take a bad situation and turn it into a competition: when life hands us lemons, we just don't make lemonade; we make lemonade-making contests. And then we make the best damned lemonade. Ever.

So that summer the first World Fuel Economy Championship was held; American midwesterner Wayne Gerdes took the top honors by squeezing 213.8 miles per gallon out of a Honda Insight. And *hypermiling*—maximizing the miles obtained per gallon of gasoline burned by changing how you drive—was selected as the best new word of the year by *The New Oxford American Dictionary*.

People began replacing their old fuel hogs with shiny and far more efficient hybrids in droves. By April of that year, sales of hybrid vehicles had peaked at forty thousand units, second only to the previous May at forty-five thousand units. At the time, this kind of upgrade probably seemed reasonable; after all, who could know that a global recession would soon crush demand, causing oil prices to collapse.

Let's think through a typical decision a not-so-typical couple might have faced back in 2008. Assume Joe and Jen each own a car, and that they each drive about the same distance each year. Joe drives a beat-up truck and is considering upgrading to something newer and a bit more fuel efficient. Jen drives a sporty compact but has her eye on a hybrid. Because they are newlyweds on a tight budget, they realize that they can only afford to buy one new vehicle. If their goal is to reduce gasoline consumption, which car should they replace? Before you make your recommendation, exhibit 9–1 provides some information about each of their current cars and the replacement vehicles they're considering.

Most people say that Jen should replace her car with the 50 mpg hybrid. After all, the improvement in her mileage figure (**20 = 50-30**) is five times greater than in Joe's ( **4 = 20-16**). But it turns out that either replacement offers about the same savings in terms of gas consumption.

| JOE'S DECISION | |
|---|---|
| Current truck | 16 mpg |
| New truck | 20 mpg |

| JEN'S DECISION | |
|---|---|
| Current coupe | 30 mpg |
| New hybrid | 50 mpg |

EXHIBIT 9-1. Fuel efficiency estimates for Joe and Jen. The panel on the left shows fuel efficiency for Joe's current truck as well as the new truck he's considering. The panel on the right shows similar information for Jen's existing coupe and the new hybrid she's considering.

Here's the math. Assume each car is driven 100 miles each week. Joe's truck gets 16 mpg, so it burns 6.3 gallons (**100 MILES ÷ 16 MPG** ). The new 20 mpg truck burns 5 gallons instead (**100 MILES ÷ 20 MPG** ), saving about 1.3 gallons (**6.3-5**) per week. Jen's coupe gets 30 mpg, burning 3.3 gallons per week (**100 MILES ÷ 30 MPG**). Upgrading to that 50 mpg hybrid would use 2 gallons per week (**100 MILES ÷ 50 MPG**) instead, for a savings of 1.3 (**3.3-2**) gallons. This difference is identical to the savings associated with upgrading Joe's far less efficient truck.

The bottom line here is that things are sometimes just flat out not the way they seem (a lesson that Joe and Jen as newlyweds are sure to learn in a broader sense). As noted by Richard Larrick and Jack Soll, authors of a paper in *Science*, this computational illusion has important policy implications: our focus on miles per gallon as the measure of efficiency misdirects our attention away from the real opportunity, which is getting Joe's old truck off the road.

Whatever. If you're like most people, your head is still spinning too much from the long division to worry about environmental policy. What you're really asking is, what's a trendy girl like Jen doing with a redneck like Joe?

Why *do* we get this problem wrong? Doesn't this just mean that math is hard?

Well, yes, math is hard, and sometimes it's downright nasty. But what's interesting here is not that getting the right answer is so hard; it's that getting the wrong answer is so easy. We're not only quick at coming to a mistaken conclusion—we're clueless that we've ended up in the wrong place.

We don't get it totally wrong, which may be part of the problem. In the example above, we understand right away that we want to compare differences: specifically, differences in efficiency between two replacement cars. So our brains jump on it and look at the differences, without stopping to consider whether the metrics were designed with taking differences in mind. (They weren't.)

Imagine that instead of reporting miles per gallon, the EPA reported gallons used per hundred miles; for simplicity, let's call that GPH. The lower the GPH, the better (i.e., less fuel required to drive a certain distance).

Now let's revisit Jen and Joe's decisions with this revamped metric. Thank goodness, we've already done that math. Exhibit 9–2 shows the same pair of decisions using the GPH metric instead of MPG.

Using different metrics makes it far easier to see that both replacements offer similar gains in terms of fuel use (about 1.3 gallons per 100 miles for either option). By the way, this is how most European countries rate the fuel efficiency of automobiles (i.e., amount of fuel required to go a fixed distance rather than distance you can go on a fixed amount of fuel).

If gallons per hundred miles is so much better as a measure of efficiency, why did we end up with miles per gallon instead?

| JOE'S DECISION | |
| --- | --- |
| Current truck | 6.3 gph |
| New truck | 5.0 gph |

| JEN'S DECISION | |
| --- | --- |
| Current coupe | 3.3 gph |
| New hybrid | 2.0 gph |

EXHIBIT 9-2. Fuel efficiency estimates for Joe and Jen using the "gallons per hundred miles" (or GPH) metric. Note that this metric makes it much easier to see that either replacement will save the same amount of fuel, assuming Joe and Jen drive the same distance.

I've asked around, and no one seems to know. One possibility, which both Professor Larrick and I arrived at independently, is that in some situations range is more important than fuel efficiency. (I speculated that the military might be more interested in how far a vehicle could go before needing to refuel; Larrick speculated that the United States is a big country and it is important to know how far a tank of gas could get you lest you be stuck on a country road.) Larrick also noted that it's easier to divide bigger numbers by smaller numbers, which also might explain statistics like "at bats per strikeout" (or AB per SO). As with miles per gallon, the AB per SO metric also exaggerates differences: a player with a 2 percent chance of striking out each time he's at bat has an AB per SO of 50, while another with a slightly higher 3 percent chance of striking out each time has an AB per SO of 33. Larrick's speculation is that people were driving and fussing over fuel efficiency long before calculators and onboard computers were cheap and available, so they calculated miles per gallon because that was just flat out easier to do. The EPA simply followed their lead.

But who knows? I asked a pilot about how airlines measure fuel efficiency and was surprised to learn that their metric is pounds of fuel per mile: that is, how many pounds of fuel you burn to fly one mile. This metric does the trick as well, because absolute differences in pounds per mile flown directly reflect genuine differences in efficiency.

More importantly, who cares? Well, I do, and I think you should, too. It implies that simple changes in the way we present choices and information can have outsized effects on the behaviors we're trying to promote.

## WHY IS EASY SO GOOD?

There are different flavors of easy. The first is probably the one that comes most quickly to mind: if we remove or lower the costs (or hassles) of the right option, people will be more likely to choose that alternative. This makes intuitive sense, but it makes even more sense in light of what we saw in chapter 2: namely, that humans are wired to be impatient. Most good behaviors that are difficult involve an up-front cost for a future benefit. If you'll recall, a good rule of thumb is that future outcomes are psychologically discounted by about half. Thus, any future benefit needs to be at least twice as big as the up-front hassle. That's why removing as many of the here-and-now hassles associated with the desired behavior can be so important.

In the setting of personal retirement savings, for example, Laibson and colleagues made it super easy for employees to join a company's 401(k) plan: all they had to do was check a box on a postcard and return it to the human resources department. Laibson and team removed the effort that each employee normally would have faced: choosing a contribution level, determining how to allocate the contribution to various funds, and the like. Importantly, they found that they could increase enrollment by about 15 percent each time they sent out the cards to employees who hadn't yet enrolled. The bottom line is that what logically looks like a small bump on the road to better behavior psychologically looks more like a wall. Thus, any time a fifty bits designer can remove a hassle or effort that people face when engaging in the desired behavior, she should consider it. Of course, that hassle doesn't magically disappear; if the person whose behavior the designer is trying to change isn't doing it, that means the designer has to figure out a way to get it done.

Another type of easy is a bit less obvious, and the neuroscientists and psychologists refer to it as *fluency*. Fluency is the ease with which our brains process incoming information. It turns out to be very important, because our brains tend to associate fluency with a bunch of other important things. The greater the fluency, the more we judge a statement to be true, the more we like it, the more we are confident about it, the more popular and prevalent we think it is, and the easier we think it is to do. It sounds as though fluency is a lot like how my dad feels about WD-40: it's good for what ails you.

It's possible to alter fluency in ways that are easier than you might expect. For example, cities whose names are printed in easier-to-read fonts are judged to be closer than those printed in hard-to-read fonts; they're also described in more concrete terms. Money with which we're unfamiliar (e.g., foreign currency) is judged to be less valuable than familiar currency; this means that all the new coins and bills introduced over the past few years by the US Treasury may have added to our spending.

Fluency can also be affected by the names we give things. Stock prices of companies with easy-to-pronounce names do a lot better on the day they go public than prices of companies that are hard to pronounce. Recipes printed in hard-to-read fonts are judged by readers to take longer to prepare than those printed in easier-to-read fonts, and roller coasters with tough-to-pronounce names are judged to be more risky to ride. On the Express Scripts website, we found that the more explanatory text we included about potential savings opportunities, the *less* successful we were at getting patients to make a change; a preliminary study found that (made-up) drugs with hard-to-pronounce names are not viewed as favorably as those with easier-to-pronounce names, which may be a built-in disadvantage for generic medications.

## WHY EASY ISN'T ALWAYS BETTER

As a result of all of this, you'd think it would be to your advantage to make the processing of information as simple as possible to improve the believability, likability, and desirability of the behavior or choice you're trying to advantage. And most of the time you'd be right. But there's an important exception: if there's a suboptimal option that is attracting people's decisions when they're on autopilot, you may be better off making *all* of the choices *more* difficult.

Here's an example, in the form of a question: *How many animals of each kind did Moses take on the Ark?* Most people answer two, even though they know that it was Noah, not Moses, who built and loaded the Ark. If Bible stories aren't your cup of frankincense or myrrh, try this one: *What was the famous line uttered by Louis Armstrong when he first set foot on the moon?* People get this one wrong, too, even though they know that Louis Armstrong is a jazz great and Neil Armstrong (no relation, I believe) was the fellow who first set foot on the moon.

Researchers have shown that they can increase the rate at which subjects give the right answer to these "trick" questions by making the font in which the riddle is printed a bit more difficult to read. They split subjects into two groups at random and had them read the question as shown in exhibit 9–3. Although only 12 percent of the group reading the question printed in the

| How many animals of each kind did Moses take on the Ark? | How many animals of each kind did Moses take on the Ark? |

EXHIBIT 9-3. Two versions of the "Moses" question. The easier-to-read version is on the left; the harder-to-read version is on the right.

easier-to-read font got the correct answer, that rate jumped to 47 percent in the group assigned to the tougher-to-read font.

Presumably, this happens because the reduced processing fluency caused by the harder-to-read font causes people to engage more of their fifty bits. In other words, insert enough disfluency, and you'll cause people to jump out of their automatic behavior to slow down and start to more carefully analyze a problem. If the desired choice is the one that people are likely to accept only after stopping and really thinking things through, you may be better off *decreasing* the fluency of the overall choice process.

The bottom line is that if your call to action can be accomplished by "riding" automatic, intuitive behaviors, then fluency is your friend. If, on the other hand, the behavior you're trying to engage requires careful consideration of a value proposition, then adding just enough disfluency to the choice process may help.

## DESIGNING WITH WISE SIMPLIFICATION

To help demonstrate how to simplify wisely, we'll use the example of a business that wants to encourage greater physical activity among employees who work at the company's headquarters. Specifically, the company would like able-bodied employees to take the stairs rather than the elevator at its soon-to-be-built new headquarters building.

The first step in wise simplification is to make the preferred choice or behavior as easy as possible, including how any information is presented. To make use of the stairs as easy as possible, we will recommend that the company make the staircase easy to find, well illuminated, and visually appealing.

Next, if you believe that people are still likely to select a nonpreferred option, consider redesigning the choice process to introduce disfluency. For our example, we suggest placing the elevators as far away from the entrance as the building, ADA, and fire codes allow, and we recommend the use of signage that requires those who are inclined to use the elevators to slow down just a bit.

If there's a way to make the right choice or behavior the easiest one, go for it. In practice, however, making the desired option easier for the decision maker generally means extra work for someone. For example, when an Express Scripts patient wants to switch his medication from a retail pharmacy to the home delivery pharmacy, he will typically need a new prescription from his physician. To make this as easy as possible, Express Scripts may offer to help by contacting the physician on the patient's behalf to obtain that prescription. Although that means a lot less work on the part of the patients, it means more work for the company.

In addition, in some situations there may be regulations or laws that make it difficult to make the best choice effortless. For example, some patients taking maintenance medications for a chronic condition—in other words, a pill that they take every day—procrastinate on getting their prescriptions renewed. One possible solution would be to obtain a prescription for a large number of refills (say, two years' worth of medications). As I understand it, however, some states don't allow pharmacies to process prescriptions with more than a year's worth of refills. In addition, we would need to determine whether and to what degree this approach might lead to dispensing medication that goes unused.

Finally, there are some aspects of a behavior that just can't be "outsourced." For example, it would be really nice if I could pay someone to exercise for me. (I suppose I could, but it wouldn't make me any more fit.) Relying solely on the "simplify wisely" strategy in those situations may not have a big enough effect.

**The main message** of this chapter is that we need to have a strong counterpoint to the general tendency—especially among digital designers—to make everything as easy as possible for users (e.g., reduce the number of clicks). That approach is fine, but it implicitly assumes that the designer lacks a point of view and the user has a clear one.

On the other hand, if you believe that behavior is not deliberate and is instead subject to drift due to inattention and inertia, then whether you make behaviors easy or hard is critical. If people are headed in the right direction, easy is your friend: use more of it; make the interactions fast and frictionless. If people are headed the wrong direction, or if it's difficult for people to know which option is best without more deliberate thought, however, then easy is probably your enemy: you want less of it, and you want people to slow down and be a bit more deliberate.

In many ways, wise simplification is at the heart of all of the other fifty bits strategies. For example, using opt-outs is the epitome of making the right thing easy; using active choice is the epitome of slowing people down so that automatically choosing the wrong thing is harder.

In the next and final chapter, we gain a better understanding of how accomplished fifty bits designers select and combine multiple strategies to solve real-world problems, and how fifty bits design differs from and complements other approaches to behavior change. We also consider some of the risks that come with fifty bits design and how best to avoid them.

# CHAPTER 10

# Forging a New Science for Better Behavior

Most of the world's religions tell us that children are a blessing, but common sense (and epidemiologic data) tell us that timing is everything. The birth of a child is a life-changing event, and unintended pregnancies—especially among teens—come at a heavy cost. Nearly all of the milestones that parents desire for their children and society wants for its members—graduating from high school, going to college, achieving financial independence, enjoying a stable relationship with a partner or spouse—are put at significant risk when a woman experiences an unplanned pregnancy. And the outcomes are equally troubling for the kids who are born as a result of these pregnancies. Unintended and mistimed pregnancies decrease the chance of obtaining prenatal care and increase the chance of premature birth and developmental problems.

Fortunately, highly effective forms of contraception offer women the opportunity to time their pregnancies, delaying the birth of their children until they and their partners are best able to care for them. This in turn increases the likelihood that women attend college, pursue advanced degrees, and enter the paid labor force. Contraception also contributes to marriages occurring later in life, offering the chance for both men and women to better understand what they want from a relationship and to find a suitable partner.

Contraceptive technology, however, has fallen short of its full potential. Half of all pregnancies in the United States are unintended—a whopping 3.4 million per year. And although all sociodemographic groups are affected by unintended pregnancies, those who can least afford it (i.e., lower-income women) are at the greatest risk.

As we saw in chapter 4, this doesn't have to be the case. Long-acting reversible contraception (IUDs and implantable hormones) are highly effective at preventing unintended pregnancies, with failure rates of less than 1 percent per year. Unfortunately, the vast majority of women who are trying to avoid getting pregnant simply don't use these methods.

The most obvious barrier to using these methods is financial: although their annualized costs are lower than other, less-effective methods (e.g., oral contraceptives), their costs are significant and occur up front. But it turns out that removing the cost barrier isn't enough. For example, California's family planning program, Family PACT, provides contraceptive services to the uninsured whose income is less than 200 percent of the federal poverty level. Despite Family PACT's eliminating out-of-pocket costs to its beneficiaries, LARC accounted for only 5.1 percent of all contraceptive methods in 2009 for that program. The Affordable Care Act (ACA) completely eliminates cost as a barrier for all women who are covered by commercial health insurance.

And although out-of-pocket costs for contraception have plummeted since that provision of the ACA has been enacted, uptake of LARC methods has barely budged.

LARC methods offer a highly effective way for women to avoid unintended pregnancies and, as a result, stay on track to have a better life for themselves and their families. Nonetheless, they're underused, and eliminating out-of-pocket costs isn't enough to significantly affect how often these methods are used. What to do? One team of researchers in St. Louis set out to change the landscape of family planning by applying several of the strategies from fifty bits design.

## THE CONTRACEPTIVE CHOICE PROJECT

In the summer of 2007, researchers at Washington University in St. Louis launched a bold project to reduce the number of unintended pregnancies in the region by offering contraception to ten thousand women of childbearing age. They believed that the most effective methods of contraception—long-acting reversible methods such as intrauterine devices and implantable hormones—were significantly underused. At the time the study was planned, less than 5 percent of contraceptives being used were LARC methods; the vast majority were methods like oral contraceptives. They hoped to increase the LARC rate to about 10 percent.

Over the next four years, the study enrolled 9,256 women. Each woman was given comprehensive information about every method available. The program—which was funded by an anonymous foundation—ensured that participants wouldn't have to pay anything out of pocket for any method they chose.

Counselors were trained to provide information to participants, and there was ample staffing to ensure that women didn't have to endure long waits to be seen. The program was designed so that each participant would receive the method she chose during the same visit in which she made she decision.

The CHOICE Project put into practice several fifty bits strategies:

- *Lock in good intentions.* Refillable methods such as oral contraceptives require a high degree of adherence to work. In contrast, LARC methods allow women to make a one-time decision to avoid unintended pregnancy; they are a technology that enables women to precommit to contraception and makes forgetting irrelevant.

- *Reframe the choices.* CHOICE used tiered counseling—a type of "order framing"—very effectively in counseling women about their contraceptive options. The researchers were surprised to find that most physicians started their discussions with women by focusing on either the method the patient was currently using or the one with which the patient was most familiar. Much of the time, this meant anchoring the discussion around oral contraceptives, which are effective but only when taken religiously. Instead, the CHOICE staff developed an approach in which all of the methods were presented in their order of effectiveness, starting with the most effective methods and working their way down to the least effective methods. The result is that effectiveness remains front and center in how women are thinking about contraception, and that any trade-offs that are made are done so in light of effectiveness.

- *Require choice.* The CHOICE project relied on trained counselors to inform participants of their options, freeing up clinical staff to focus on inserting LARC methods for women who chose them. This approach meant that women could receive their method the same day that they made their decision. Although participants were not absolutely required to make a decision during their visit, removing the delay between making a selection and receiving their method effectively bridged the gap between their contraceptive intentions and the method they received.

- *Simplify wisely.* This is an area in which CHOICE was exceptional. The staff was fully trained to put the participant at the center of the experience. They removed every barrier to obtaining the most effective method of each participant's choice. They removed all financial obstacles and completely reworked the clinic experience to ensure that each participant left her visit with the method she wanted. They provided extensive in-person and phone-based support throughout the study so that women with questions or concerns could have them addressed as quickly as possible. For example, rather than requiring participants to return to the clinic for their annual chlamydia and gonorrhea screening, the program provided in-home tests for sexually transmitted infections that the women could perform themselves. But the CHOICE staff didn't just make everything easy. In simplifying wisely, they insisted that every participant receive comprehensive counseling about all of the contraceptive methods. This requirement helped ensure that participants were engaging their fifty bits in deciding which method they'd use.

The result of CHOICE's application of these fifty bits strategies is jaw-dropping. Use of LARC methods among participants soared to 75 percent. The vast majority of women who chose LARC methods stuck with them—including teens. Repeat abortions dropped in the St. Louis region, while they rose in Kansas City (the control comparator). Rates of pregnancy, birth, and abortion among teens in the CHOICE project were a staggering 75 percent lower than among similar teens across the United States as a whole. At three years, over 80 percent of participants were still active in the study—an exceptionally high retention rate. It was by every measure an extraordinary success.

The CHOICE Project is a powerful example of how an entire experience can be reengineered to unlock the good intentions that most people already have. Participants in the CHOICE Project had every intention of preventing unintended pregnancies but all too often experienced outcomes at odds with those intentions. By employing multiple fifty bits strategies—precommitment, reframing, active choice, wise simplification—the leaders of the CHOICE Project were exceptionally effective in reducing unintended pregnancies. They became fifty bits designers.

## MAKING THE MOST OF FIFTY BITS DESIGN

You might be wondering when to use each of the fifty bits design strategies. The practice of fifty bits design is still somewhat new,

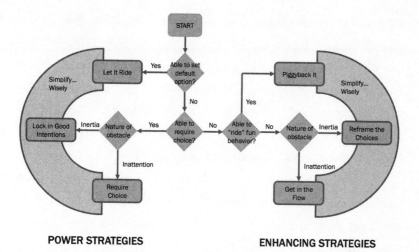

EXHIBIT 10-1. Flow chart to help fifty bits designers decide which lever to start with when tackling a specific application. See text for a discussion of the implications of the physical layout of the flow chart.

but experience to date suggests a set of questions that can help determine which of the strategies is likely to be the best suited for any specific application you might be considering. Exhibit 10–1 captures as a flow chart the strategies I suggest you use in different circumstances. As you work your way through the chart, you will arrive at a single suggested strategy.

A careful look at the flow chart reveals a couple of important points. First, the chart prioritizes the use of the "power" strategies, at least when they are suitable. In other words, if it's possible to use those strategies, the chart will suggest that you start there. Second, the chart helps you think about the nature of the main obstacle that keeps people from engaging in the desired choice or behavior. If the issue is inattention, one strategy will be suggested; if it's inertia, another will be suggested. Together, these two points (prioritizing the use of the power strategies over the enabling strategies, and inattention versus inertia as the main obstacle) drive the physical layout of the flow chart. The power strategies show up on the left side of the chart, and the enhancing strategies on the right. Strategies that leverage inertia appear toward the top of the flow chart, and those that address inattention appear toward the bottom. The über strategy of making the right choices easy and the wrong ones hard appears as curved bands spanning the other two sets of strategies.

As we've just seen, the strategies are most powerful when they are combined, and—at least at this point in time—how to combine them is as much an act of trial and error as of science. That said, it's very useful to look to the flow chart for guidance about the core strategy on which a solution should be based, then layer on additional strategies as suitable to drive better behavior.

## GUARDRAILS

Fifty bits design is based on a set of seven strategies that produce positive change while preserving individual choice. These strategies work because of the psychological realities that are inherent to being human. Once we understand these underlying forces and the available strategies, we can combine them in countless ways to promote specific behaviors.

Applying fifty bits design comes with some temptations and pitfalls, however, and therefore some responsibilities. After all, the interests of designers and those of people exposed to those designs may not be fully aligned at every point in time and for every issue. Some choices and behaviors might make the designer (or the organization for whom the designer works) better off at the expense of the decision maker. In short, without some guiding principles, fifty bits design could be nothing more than "trickonomics."

I don't know what kind of trouble you'll run into as you apply fifty bits design at work or at home. (Hopefully you won't run into any, but if you do, I'd like to hear about it and what you learned.) In general, though, here are a few recommendations to help you get the most from fifty bits design while keeping your nose clean.

### Clearly Define Success, and Then Do the "Mom" Test

Be straightforward about what you're trying to achieve. Write out in plain language the behavior you're trying to encourage. Now imagine reading aloud what you just wrote to your mother, including it in your family holiday card, or seeing it printed tomorrow morning on the front page of the *New York Times*. If you cringe, rethink your goal.

### Avoid Deception

These two simple words will save you a world of hurt. Simply put, ask yourself whether a reasonable person armed with all the facts would feel deceived by anything you're doing to advantage one behavior over another. This imaginary person doesn't have to agree with you to clear this hurdle but should—on reflection—understand why you did what you did.

### Be Intellectually Honest

Fifty bits design is important and powerful, but it's not magic. Some of the applications you'll try will disappoint you. Some will flop completely. Many interventions won't have the outsized effect that setting the default did in 401(k) plans, but in many situations a far more modest effect is still material. We're in the earliest stages of the application of the behavioral sciences. We haven't yet completely cracked the code, and it's likely to be a while before we do. Until then, invest in a test-and-learn framework so you can confirm that the old chestnuts work and can put new ideas to the test. You could be the next Thomas Edison of behavior.

## FIFTY BITS DESIGN, DIGITAL INTERACTIONS, AND BIG DATA

All seven strategies can be applied just as effectively online as they can in the physical world. It's critical that interaction designers remember that users' brains aren't wired for endless attention, nor do they house a bottomless desire for decision making. As with other experiences, digital interactions can leverage one or more of the seven fifty bits strategies.

In some ways, however, digital interactions are superior to other types of experiences for two reasons. First, it's often easier for a digital designer to fiddle with the user interaction, and many of the fifty bits strategies involve reengineering that process. For example, an online merchant might want (but not require) customers to provide a telephone number in case of a problem with the delivery of their order. Stopping the checkout process to verify whether or not the user wants to provide a phone number will help make sure that people don't skip over that option inadvertently.

Second, and perhaps most importantly, tracking behaviors and measuring outcomes are often easier with digital interactions.

The ability to quickly and reliably test and learn is critical for getting the most from fifty bits design. For example, an online music store could randomize new customers to either active choice about whether to have their monthly subscription automatically renewed or an opt-out program in which their monthly subscription is automatically renewed until the consumer deactivates it. The capability to randomize and measure differences between approaches allows fifty bits designers to more quickly optimize the programs and solutions they develop.

Measurement—whether done online or in the real world—generates lots of data. The growing availability of a wide variety of personalized information enables a potentially powerful marriage between fifty bits design and "big data" (i.e., advanced analytics applied to rich sets of information).

Fifty bits design is a powerful complement to big data. Most big-data approaches to individual behavior change focus on targeting (i.e., which people to intervene on) and tailoring (i.e., which intervention to use on a subset of people). However, the interventions used typically come from classical marketing (e.g., persuasion and special offers). Fifty bits solutions offer an entirely new set of interventions designed to activate the good intentions that most people already have.

Similarly, big data is a powerful complement to fifty bits design. Using advanced analytical methods offers the possibility of determining which of the fifty bits strategies (or combination of strategies) is likely to be most effective at the level of the individual person. In short, fifty bits design can improve the power of big data by extending the interventions it can deploy, and big data can improve the effectiveness of fifty bits design by using evidence to guide its more effective application at the individual level.

A good example of the fruitful interplay between big data and fifty bits design is a program to tackle the problem of medication nonadherence. Developed by Express Scripts, *ScreenRx* combines the power of fifty bits design with that of big data.

Taking the fifty bits design perspective was critical for dealing with nonadherence because it caused us to focus on how inattention and inertia can drive this behavior. Once you understand that people are plagued by inattention and inertia, the roles of forgetting and procrastinating in driving nonadherence rise in importance. Indeed, as noted earlier, we found that nearly 70 percent of nonadherence was caused by forgetting (to take the medication, to get a refill, or to get a new prescription when needed) or procrastinating (on getting a refill or a new prescription).

But knowing the causes of nonadherence was only part of the solution. It turns out that people's adherence behavior naturally waxes and wanes over time. Specifically, 15 percent to 25 percent of people who are nonadherent during one time period will become adherent in the next . . . without any intervention. Similarly, 15 percent to 25 percent of people who *are* adherent during one time period will become nonadherent in the next. In other words, focusing interventions on patients who had been nonadherent in the past would be inefficient: a chunk of them would get better without any help (which means the intervention is a waste of time and effort), and another chunk would benefit from the intervention but don't get it.

Big data helped with this wrinkle. At the core of ScreenRx is a set of predictive models based on highly sophisticated analyses of robust datasets (i.e., big data). These models are critical because they estimate with an exceptionally high degree of accuracy the chance that any individual patient will be nonadherent to his or her prescription medications over the next twelve months. Specifically, they can identify patients who are currently adherent to therapy but at increased risk of becoming nonadherent, as well as those who are currently nonadherent but likely to become adherent even if left alone. This marriage of big-data analytics and fifty bits design allows Express Scripts to focus resources on the patients who are most likely to run into trouble, and then to intervene in a manner that unlocks the good intentions most patients already have.

Here's how the program works. Express Scripts reaches out to at-risk patients (i.e., those who have "screened positive" for nonadherence) to identify potential adherence obstacles. As expected from the fifty bits perspective, most patients have good intentions that are not being fully acted upon. Threats to their adherence are mainly due to forgetting and procrastinating, so the most effective solution is to activate their underlying good intentions via precommitment. Patients who are likely to forget to take their medications are offered simple devices that remind them when it's time to take their medications. Refill procrastinators are offered enrollment into home delivery, with automatic refills if they'd like. When cost is a concern and a lower-cost option is available, the program works with the patient's physician to get a new prescription. When nonadherence is linked to a clinical concern (e.g., the medication isn't working, it may be causing side effects, or the patient doesn't understand how to take it), the company's specialist pharmacists are on hand.

## A BETTER WAY TO BETTER BEHAVIOR

Improving human behavior—whether our own or that of others—has been a goal of a number of disciplines for a very long time. Each of these fields assumes that a different issue is at the root of suboptimal behavior, and that leads each to propose a different solution. For educators the fundamental challenge is seen as a lack of understanding; the solution is better education. For classical economists the issue is weak incentives and perhaps information asymmetry; the solution is stronger incentives and a balancing out of information. For marketers the problem is misplaced intentions of consumers; the solution is clever cajoling so as to ignite a desire that didn't exist before. For many religious leaders the trouble is our sinful nature or weak moral fiber; the solution is submission to a higher power and adherence to a strict set of rules.

Fifty bits design takes a starkly different path, and in doing so offers a bold set of new solutions for improving behavior. It rejects the assumptions that we are poorly educated, hoodwinked by others who are in the know, inadequately incentivized, resistant to change, or of questionable moral character. Instead, fifty bits design rests on a single scientific reality: our brains are the products of evolution, and as a result they are adapted for an environment that in many ways no longer exists. All too frequently, our brains act like fish out of water. Unfortunately, the natural inclinations that served us so well in a time long ago and a place far away now routinely lead us astray. Today's world demands deeper attention and more frequent decision making, but our brains are instead wired for inattention and inertia. These limitations lead to a persistent gap between our internal intentions and our outward actions.

Because it identifies a completely different cause of self-defeating behaviors, fifty bits design offers a completely new set of solutions. In contrast to other approaches, fifty bits design recognizes that most people have good intentions. For most of us, this point of view resonates deeply: we want to save more money, eat right, exercise more, be more charitable, and the like. The problem is that these good intentions all too often lie dormant. Thus, the goal of fifty bits design isn't to change people's minds. Instead, fifty bits design works by activating the good intentions that already exist. And as we've seen, this new set of strategies is exceptionally effective.

I have been using fifty bits design for several years and am still surprised at how effective its strategies are for improving behavior. Effectiveness alone is enough for me to be an enthusiastic proponent. But there is another significant advantage to putting fifty bits design to work: it assumes the best about people. It's much more optimistic and far less cynical than persuasion-based approaches to behavior change such as telemarketing and unsolicited direct (i.e., junk) mail. There are no tricks or secrets, just a deep-rooted belief that most people want to do the right thing and that they need a bit of help acting on those good intentions.

Importantly, fifty bits design is not only better for those to whom the designs are applied; it's better for the designers, too. Working with a deeper understanding of what makes us tick and with this much more hopeful, positive view of our underlying intentions leads not only to more effective means for changing behavior but to far more rewarding work for ourselves. Think about it: as a behavior change professional, would you rather get up every morning and face a long day of arm-twisting or one in which you're helping people bring their best intentions to life? In your home life, would you rather engage in a battle of wills or reengineer your environment to help your loved ones make decisions that serve their longer-term interests? And as you work to improve your own behavior, would you rather be saddled with the notion that you don't have enough self-discipline or encouraged by the fact that most of the time your intentions are well placed?

**If we are** to make any headway at all in solving the world's most pressing problems, we must make significant strides in unleashing better human behavior. Our representative democracies rely on citizens getting up off the couch and voting. Our health depends on engaging in a more active style of living, a more balanced approach to what we eat and drink, and the more effective use of proven medical interventions. Our future selves, our children, and our grandchildren are counting on us to be good stewards of the environment that we are leaving to them. Our communities need us to be more plugged in, vocal, and participatory. Our interpersonal relationships require that we more actively attend to our loved ones, even if that comes at a cost to our contributions at work.

Better behavior is mission critical for everything that matters to us as individuals, families, organizations, communities, and as a species. My deep hope and strong belief is that fifty bits design will be an important part of our success.

# Acknowledgments

Many thanks to my colleagues at Express Scripts, especially those on the Research and New Solutions teams. Special thanks go to Mark Bini, who led our innovation group through thick and thin, and to Sharon Frazee, whose many objective analyses helped convince us that we were on the right track.

Without forward-thinking clients, our program development efforts wouldn't have gotten very far. I'm especially thankful to Bob Ihrie for being an early adopter of Select Home Delivery, and to Roger Merrill for constantly encouraging us to excel in our pursuit of better health for patients.

The hidden hand behind much of my work at Express Scripts is Larry Zarin. Coach, boss, co-conspirator and friend, Larry taught me the strategic power of storytelling, the importance of not overshooting the target, and what perseverance looks like up close. Larry's fingerprints can be found throughout the book but are especially evident in the chapter on reframing.

The process of writing this book left many friends and family in its wake. I am grateful for the ongoing assistance and thoughtful feedback from Dan Ariely, Wayne Bouchardt, Christina Buckel, Mark Engel, Brad Epstein, Peter Kennedy, David Laibson (who also originally described to me the mathematics of procrastination), Chris Mayer, Bonnie Mann, Steve Miller, Jason Olsen, Peter Orszag, Ron Pipes, Sarah Proehl, Sandy Schenk, Glen Stettin, Jenny and Chris Stockburger, Tim Wentworth, and Howard Weissman. David Bragg and Meghan Weingrad made terrific suggestions about the framework for the seven strategies for which I am most grateful.

My father, Bob Nease Sr., encouraged my curiosity at every turn for as long as I can recall. He was also relentless in correcting my grammar but no less vigorous with his constant support as this book came together. I am also thankful for the strong and well-timed words of encouragement from Helen Darling, Dan Gilbert, and Virginia O'Brien.

Buckets of gratitude also go to my energetic and effective agent, Giles Anderson, who saw a potential book in the mess that was an early draft, and to the terrific Hollis Heimbouch at HarperCollins, whose straightforward guidance made the book much more readable.

Special thanks go to my sons, Bobby and Billy, for patiently engaging in countless discussions about behavioral sciences over many years. I am also very thankful to my father-in-law, Ron Secura, who kept me well fed and in good spirits across two continents during the tail end of this project.

Gina, words fall so very far short. Thank you for not just indulging me in chasing my dreams but helping to make so many of them come true. (Thanks also for keeping the dogs out of my hair during those long stretches of research and writing.) You're my best friend and my perfect fit. Here's to what I hope is a long road ahead of us, full of adventures.

*The Power of Fifty Bits* has been nourished and propelled by lots of people named and unnamed here. That said, any errors or omissions fall squarely in my lap.

# Notes

**INTRODUCTION**

xvii Jack's bad behavior at that portentous dinner: I've shared this story with many people, and as a result have received many suggestions about how to put an end to Jack-like dinner behavior. Classical economists tend to suggest that each diner pay his or her own way. Ethicists and anthropologists often argue that Jack should be warned that unless he changes his ways, he will be shunned from future dinners. Psychologists sometimes suggest that one person pick up the entire tab, with that responsibility rotating among participants. But one of my favorite suggestions came from a man who doesn't drink alcohol. After growing tired of subsidizing the hefty wine and cocktail tab of his fellow diners despite his protests, he ordered an entire cake for dessert, had a slice, and then had the remainder boxed up to take home. He told me he's never had to share in the cost of booze since.

xix User-centered design focuses on making things easy: It's hard to nail down a definition of user-centered design on which all of its practitioners agree. The point of view I've articulated is consistent with that previously described by Donald Norman (see D. A. Norman, "Cognitive Engineering," in *User Centered Systems Design*, ed. D. A. Norman and S. W. Draper [Hillsdale, NJ: Lawrence Erlbaum Associates, 1986]).

## CHAPTER 1. WIRED FOR INATTENTION AND INERTIA

3    Ten million bits per second is: The estimate of ten million bits per second as the total throughput of the brain is based primarily on the total number of neurons delivering information to the brain from the senses (vision, touch, hearing, taste, and smell). The bandwidth required for visual processing is approximately ten million bits per second (K. Koch, J. McLean, R. Segev, M. A. Freed, M. J. Berry II, V. Balasubramanian, and P. Sterling, "How Much the Eye Tells the Brain," *Current Biology* 16, no. 14 (2006): 1428–34) and makes up the bulk of the estimate. Another million bits per second are allotted to handling information flowing to the brain from neurons in the skin; neurons devoted to hearing, taste, and smell are far fewer and thus account for less of the overall amount of information handled by the brain. Thus the estimate of ten million bits per second for the total throughput of the brain is likely a slight underestimate. Measuring the bandwidth of the conscious mind is even more difficult. In *The User Illusion: Cutting Consciousness Down to Size* (New York: Penguin Non-Classics, 1999), Tor Nørretranders marshals evidence from multiple studies, most of which were done no later than the early 1960s. The studies measured how quickly people handle conscious processing tasks (e.g., ability to distinguish various stimuli, or the maximum speed with which people could interpret symbols). The conscious processing speed from these studies ranged from two bits per second to forty-four bits per second. Thus, fifty bits per second is at the upper end of the estimates reported by Nørretranders and therefore may be an overestimate. Fortunately, the arguments and insights laid out in *The Power of Fifty Bits* hold even if either estimate is off by one or two orders of magnitude. The conscious portion of the human brain is simply not capable of keeping track of everything that is occurring nor of making rational decisions on a full-time basis. For a powerful description of these issues, see Daniel Kahneman's book *Thinking, Fast and Slow* (New York: Farrar, Straus & Giroux, 2011).

3    we tend to focus our attention on things that are either pressing or pleasurable: The brain's fifty bits limitation can also cause a completely different kind of problem, one that leads to sleepless nights—or worse—for millions of us. Rumination happens when we misappropriate our scarce fifty bits of attention to ponder what might have been or what might come to pass despite our inability to change the past and our limited ability to shape the future. Sadly, these self-initiated recursive thoughts can get in the way of more healthy experiences, and when amplified are associated with clinically significant depression. If rumination is keeping

you up at night, here's something that might help. The trick is to leverage the fact that your mind has only fifty bits with which to work: get it engaged in something other than what's keeping you up and you're likely to quickly fall asleep. To do this, start working on an artificial, low-stakes problem. The one that works best for me is to imagine each letter of the Pledge of Allegiance being typed or handwritten—one letter at a time, in as great detail as possible. It's very difficult to fully attend to this task and engage in any other mental work (i.e., worrying about something else). If you find your mind has wandered back to the original problem that's keeping you awake, stop and go back to the very start of the pledge. This method for breaking the rumination cycle works by leveraging the inherent cognitive limitation we all experience: if we point our fifty bits at a harmless problem, we have no bandwidth left to deploy to whatever issue is keeping us awake.

3    John Lennon: Although Lennon's song "Beautiful Boy (Darling Boy)" includes the lines "Life is what happens to you / When you are busy making other plans" the earliest use is attributed to Allen Saunders in the January 1957 edition of *Reader's Digest* magazine.

6    nonadherence was completely accidental: For details see S. G. Frazee, S. B. Miller, R. Nease, and G. Stettin, *2011 Drug Trend Report*, Express Scripts Research & New Solutions Lab, April 2012.

7    "a camping trip that lasted an entire lifetime": Leda Cosmides and John Tooby offer an excellent and accessible primer on evolutionary psychology, available at http://www.cep.ucsb.edu/primer.html.

7    consider the things that spook us: For data on deaths from snakebites, see A. Kasturiratne, A. R. Wickremasinghe, N. de Silva, N. K. Gunawardena, A. Pathmeswaran, R. Premaratna, L. Savioli, D. G. Lalloo, and H. J. de Silva, "The Global Burden of Snakebite: A Literature Analysis and Modelling Based on Regional Estimates of Envenoming and Deaths," *PLoS Medicine*, November 4, 2008, doi:10.1371/journal .pmed.0050218. The estimate of deaths due to spider bites is based on R. L. Langley, "Animal Bites and Stings Reported by United States Poison Control Centers, 2001–2005," *Wilderness Environental Medicine* 19, no. 1 (2008): 7–14. Data on bicycle fatalities were obtained from US Department of Transportation, "Traffic Safety Facts, 2010 Data: Bicyclists and Other Cyclists," DOT HS 811 624, June 2012. Estimates of deaths from heart disease are taken from Centers for Disease Control and Prevention, "FastStats: Leading Causes of Death," http://www.cdc.gov/nchs/fastats /lcod.htm, as accessed December 26, 2012.

8   Our standard of living was stuck in the mud: Gregory Clark's somewhat controversial but fascinating *A Farewell to Alms: A Brief Economic History of the World* (Princeton, NJ: Princeton University Press, 2007) provides a compelling picture of the profound shift in economics and social welfare that occurred as a result of the industrial revolution.

9   Predictably irrational or living logically: Dan Ariely's *Predictably Irrational: The Hidden Forces That Shape Our Decisions* (New York: HarperCollins, 2008) lays out the argument that humans behave irrationally in reliable ways and includes a description of the "hot state/cool state" findings regarding sexual behaviors. Tim Harford's *The Logic of Life* (New York: Random House, 2008) focuses on how many behaviors appear logical once one understands the incentives at work, including the discussion about how sexual behaviors among teenagers appears to respond to nonfinancial costs.

12  brain is one of the most energy-intensive organs: For more details, see Nikhil Swaminathan, "Why Does the Brain Need So Much Power?" *Scientific American*, April 29, 2008, http://www.scientificamerican.com /article.cfm?id=why-does-the-brain-need-s, and M. E. Raichle and D. A. Gusnard, "Appraising the Brain's Energy Budget," *Proceedings of the National Academy of Sciences* 99, no. 16 (2002): 10237–39.

13  cheat . . . when the room was dimly lit: See C.B. Zhong, V. K. Bohns, and F. Gino, "Good Lamps Are the Best Police: Darkness Increases Dishonesty and Self-Interested Behavior," *Psychological Science* 21, no. 3 (2010): 311–14 for the details of this fascinating study.

15  Priming . . . alter people's choices: The Belgian employment findings are reported in F. Anseel and W. Duyck, "Unconscious Applicants: A Systematic Test of the Name-Letter Effect," *Psychological Science* 19, no. 10 (2008): 1059–61. B. W. Pelham, M. C. Mirenberg, and J. T. Jones provide startling evidence about how small factors associated with how we see ourselves (e.g., our names) have measurable effects on what we do for a living and where we do it in "Why Susie Sells Seashells by the Seashore: Implicit Egotism and Major Life Decisions," *Journal of Personality and Social Psychology* 82, no. 4 (2002): 469–87. The study linking feelings of hunger, generosity, and poverty is reported in B. Briers, M. Pandelaere, S. Dewitte, and L. Warlop, "Hungry for Money: The Desire for Caloric Resources Increases the Desire for Financial Resources and Vice Versa," *Psychological Science* 17, no. 11 (2006): 939–43. For an interesting overview of unconscious behavior, including priming, see John Bargh's chapter entitled "Bypassing the Will" in *The New Unconscious*, edited by R. R. Hassin, J. S. Uleman, and J. A. Bargh (New York: Oxford University Press, 2006).

## CHAPTER 2. BEHAVIORAL SHORTCUTS

20  our behaviors today reflect three shortcuts: These three shortcuts reflect overall tendencies within a population rather than deterministic rules that apply to all individuals. Clearly, some people demonstrate behaviors that fly in the face of these general shortcuts: some people don't care a bit about whether or how they fit into the group, others invite risks, and others manage to treat future outcomes as being as important as those in the present, or even more important. In fact, some of the most successful people violate one or more of these shortcuts: the visionary doesn't care too much about fitting in, isn't afraid to lose everything in pursuit of the goal, and will accept steep costs in the present for future success. When taken to the extreme, however, each of these deviations from the general rule becomes pathological: the person becomes a sociopath, has a death wish, or is completely detached from the present. In a very real sense, these are the exceptions that prove the rules.

20  buying a Prius: See M. Maynard, "Say 'Hybrid' and Many People Will Hear 'Prius,'" *New York Times*, July 4, 2007, http://www .nytimes.com/2007/07/04/business/04hybrid.html.

21  Prius sales that were due to the green "halo" effect: For the details on this clever study, see S. E. Sexton and A. L. Sexton, "Conspicuous Conservation: The Prius Halo and Willingness to Pay for Environmental Bona Fides," *Journal of Environmental Economics and Management* 67, no. 3 (2014): 303–17.

21  geographic variation in the fraction of people who "lean green": Presidential election results for Boulder County and Weld County are from "2012 Colorado Presidential Results," *Politco*, http://www.politico. com/2012-election/results/president/colorado/. For more on the association between political affiliation and attitudes about the environment, see M. E. Kahn, "Do Greens Drive Hummers or Hybrids? Environmental Ideology as a Determinant of Consumer Choice and the Aggregate Ecological Footprint," *Social Science Research Network*, http://papers.ssrn.com /sol3/papers.cfm?abstract_id=940033.

23  eCookie Project: See the 2012 annual report of the Girl Scouts USA for more information on this effort.

26  people generally have a much more difficult time: The problems discussed here are a type of *Wason selection task*. Such tasks have long been used to test the mechanisms people use to reason through problems. Leda Cosmides and John Tooby employed multiple variants of these tasks to show that most people are able to detect potential cheaters but not nearly as

good when the tasks involve sterile logic. For more on their work, see L. Cosmides, "Deduction or Darwinian Algorithms? An Explanation of the 'Elusive' Content Effect on the Wason Selection Task" (PhD diss., Harvard University, 1985), University Microfilms 86–02206; L. Cosmides, "The Logic of Social Exchange: Has Natural Selection Shaped How Humans Reason? Studies with the Wason Selection Task," *Cognition* 3, no. 31 (1989): 187–276; L. Cosmides and J. Tooby, "Evolutionary Psychology and the Generation of Culture, Part II: Case Study: A Computational Theory of Social Exchange," *Ethology and Sociobiology* 10, no. 3 (1989): 51–97; and L. Cosmides and J. Tooby, "Cognitive Adaptations for Social Exchange," in *The Adapted Mind: Evolutionary Psychology and the Generation of Culture*, edited by J. H. Barkow, L. Cosmides, and J. Tooby (New York: Oxford University Press, 1992), 163–228.

30  depending on whether outcomes were framed as gains or losses: For one of the earliest and most influential reports on this effect, see Amos Tversky and Daniel Kahneman, "The Framing of Decisions and the Psychology of Choice," *Science* 21, no. 4481 (1981): 453–58.

31  professional golfers exhibit loss aversion: For a very detailed report on this analysis, see D. G. Pope and M. E. Schweitzer, "Is Tiger Woods Loss Averse? Persistent Bias in the Face of Experience, Competition, and High Stakes," *Social Science Research Network*, June 13, 2009, http://papers.ssrn .com/sol3/papers.cfm?abstract_id=1419027.

32  Loss aversion relative to a salient goal: See D. Pope and U. Simonsohn, "Round Numbers as Goals: Evidence from Baseball, SAT Takers, and the Lab," *Psychological Science* 22, no. 1 (2011): 71–79.

32  bronze medalists appeared happier than silver medalists: For more on this fascinating study, see V. H. Medvec, S. F. Madey, and T. Gilovich, "When Less Is More: Counterfactual Thinking and Satisfaction Among Olympic Medalists," *Journal of Personality and Social Psychology* 69, no. 4 (1995): 603–10.

34  home workout gear . . . access to fitness equipment: The *Consumer Reports* survey of owners of home workout equipment was published in August 2011 and is entitled "By the Numbers: Home Exercise Machines." For more on the study of the effects of access to fitness equipment on exercise behaviors, see D. M. Williams, B. A. Lewis, S. Dunsiger, J. A. Whiteley, G. D. Papandonatos, M. A. Napolitano, B. C. Bock, J. T. Ciccolo, and B. H. Marcus, "Comparing Psychosocial Predictors of Physical Activity Adoption and Maintenance," *Annals of Behavioral Medicine* 36, no. 2 (2008): 186–94.

36   discount rate, the US government: As noted, to make sense economically
     lower discount rates may be required for long-term projects that benefit
     future generations. Just as compounding can turn a small investment into
     a big nest egg over time, benefits that occur far in the future are signifi-
     cantly diminished when even a modest discount rate is used to determine
     the equivalent value in the present. The result is that—from an economic
     perspective—programs with very large benefits far in the future are dif-
     ficult to justify when the costs of those programs occur in the present.
     For the US government's directions on discount rates to use, see Office
     of Management and Budget, Circular A–4, September 17, 2003, http://
     www.whitehouse.gov/omb/circulars_a004_a-4/.

37   hyperbolic discounting: In most financial situations, the discount rate is
     considered to be a constant value over time (e.g., 4 percent). In hyperbolic
     discounting, the discount rate declines over time in the shape of a hyper-
     bolic curve. For a detailed (and somewhat mathematically hefty) expla-
     nation, see the breakthrough article by David Laibson, "Golden Eggs and
     Hyperbolic Discounting," *Quarterly Journal of Economics* 112, no. 2 (1997):
     443–78.

39   the limbic system lights up: See S. M. McClure, D. I. Laibson, G. Loe-
     wenstein, and J. D. Cohen, "Separate Neural Systems Value Immediate
     and Delayed Monetary Rewards," *Science* 306, no. 5695 (2004): 503–7.

## CHAPTER 3. REQUIRE CHOICE

44   zero gave the state to Obama: Of the seventeen news companies that made
     state-by-state predictions, one gave Indiana to McCain, seven leaned Re-
     publican without making a call, and nine deemed the race a toss-up.

45   a particularly rough patch for the US economy: For details on the eco-
     nomic downturn of 2007 to 2011, see data available from the US Depart-
     ment of Labor Bureau of Labor Statistics at http://data.bls.gov/timeseries
     /LNS14000000 and the US Department of Commerce Bureau of Eco-
     nomic Analysis at http://www.bea.gov/national/. The decline in charitable
     giving was reported in M. Nichols, "U.S. Charitable Giving Approaches
     $300 Billion in 2011," *Reuters*, June 19, 2012, http://www.reuters.com
     /article/2012/06/19/us-usa-charity-idUSBRE85I05T20120619.

45   PetSmart Charities: For a striking view of how successful PetSmart Char-
     ities was in the face of the recent economic recession, compare its 2011
     annual report to its 2007 annual report. Despite this impressive increase,
     individual contributions to the organization in 2012 (as noted in the
     annual report) fell slightly to $39.9 million. It's unclear the degree to

which the point-of-sale campaign to "help save homeless pets" contributes to total individual contributions.

50  beloved office candy dish: Wansink's work strongly suggests that much of our eating behavior happens below our conscious awareness and is shaped by misperceptions. For details on the candy dish study, see B. Wansink, J. E. Painter, and Y.-K. Lee, "The Office Candy Dish: Proximity's Influence on Estimated and Actual Consumption," *International Journal of Obesity* 30, no. 5 (2006): 871–75.

## CHAPTER 4. LOCK IN GOOD INTENTIONS

60  SMarT . . . the opportunity to precommit: See S. Benartzi and R. Thaler, "Save More Tomorrow: Using Behavioral Economics to Increase Employee Saving," *Social Science Research Network*, January 26, 2004, http://papers.ssrn.com/abstract=489693.

60  allowing students to set their own deadlines: The fact that the majority of students chose to self-impose a deadline provides additional evidence that—at least in some settings—people are aware of the gap between their intentions and their likely actions, especially for behaviors that offer a future benefit at a cost in the near term. That the students didn't choose the optimal timing for their own deadlines suggests either that they are unaware that the timing they chose wasn't optimal or that the timing they selected was a compromise between the desires of their present and future selves. For details on the study, see D. Ariely and K. Wertenbroch, "Procrastination, Deadlines, and Performance: Self-Control by Precommitment," *Psychological Science* 13, no. 3 (2002): 219–24.

64  fiftieth anniversary of the FDA's approval of hormonal contraception: See N. Gibbs, "The Pill at 50: Sex, Freedom and Paradox," *Time*, April 22, 2010.

64  Failure rate for oral contraceptives: Oral contraceptives are very effective, but only when taken as prescribed. Adherence to oral contraceptives is more difficult than adherence to many other prescription medications; the pill should be taken at the same time every day, without fail. For estimates of failure rates for real-world use of oral contraceptives (including recent data from a large community-based study), see K. Kost, S. Singh, B. Vaughan, J. Trussell, and A. Bankole, "Estimates of Contraceptive Failure from the 2002 National Survey of Family Growth," *Contraception* 77, no. 1 (2008): 10–21; and B. Winner, J. F. Peipert, Q. Zhao, C. Buckel, T. Madden, J. E. Allsworth, and G. M. Secura, "Effectiveness of Long-Acting Reversible Contraception," *New England Journal of Medicine* 366, no. 21 (2012): 1998–2007.

65  LARC . . . a technical workaround to the fifty bits problems of inat-
    tention: See R. F. Nease, S. Glave Frazee, L. Zarin, and S. B. Miller,
    "Choice Architecture Is a Better Strategy than Engaging Patients to
    Spur Behavior Change," *Health Affairs (Millwood)* 32, no. 2 (2013): 242–
    49. We also argue in this paper that patient engagement is a very tall
    order due to the fifty bits problems of inattention and inertia, and urge
    deeper consideration of strategies that activate the good intentions that
    most patients already have.

68  StickK.com . . . success rates: These results were provided via personal
    communication from Jordan Goldberg, StickK.com LLC's CEO (May
    22, 2013).

73  default precommitment option: See J. D. Goldhaber-Fiebert, E. Blu-
    menkranz, and A. M. Garber, "Committing to Exercise: Contract
    Design for Virtuous Habit Formation," [Internet]. National Bureau of
    Economic Research Working Paper 16624, December 2010, http://
    www.nber.org/papers/w16624. This study is a good example of how
    fifty bits strategies can be combined; in this case precommitment is the
    overarching strategy, with contract length set to a default (i.e., opt-out)
    duration.

**CHAPTER 5. LET IT RIDE**

75  domino exchange: M. Wollan, "The Great American Kidney Swap,"
    *New York Times*, April 4, 2015, http://www.nytimes.com/2015/05/03
    /magazine/the-great-american-kidney-swap.html.

79  Few employees followed through: See J. J. Choi, D. Laibson, B. C.
    Madrian, and A. Metrick, "Defined Contribution Pensions: Plan Rules,
    Participant Decisions, and the Path of Least Resistance," National Bureau
    of Economic Research Working Paper 8655, December 2001, http://
    www.nber.org/papers/w8655.

81  making the right choice the default: See R. F. Nease, S. Glave Frazee, L.
    Zarin, and S. B. Miller, "Choice Architecture Is a Better Strategy than
    Engaging Patients to Spur Behavior Change," *Health Affairs (Millwood)* 32,
    no. 2 (2013): 242–49.

86  When should we use active choice and when should we use opt-out?:
    Although it gets at the main issues, the rule of thumb presented here rests
    on simplifying assumptions. For a more thorough examination of how
    to balance the potential costs and benefits of these two approaches, visit
    www.fiftybits.com.

**CHAPTER 6. GET IN THE FLOW**

90 Breakfast cereal is big business: See A. De Angelis, "General Mills and Kelloggs Continue to Dominate the US Breakfast Cereals Market," *Companies and Markets*, April 29, 2013, http://www.com paniesandmarkets.com/News/Food-and-Drink/General-Mills-and -Kelloggs-continue-to-dominate-the-US-breakfast-cereals-market /NI7060.

90 Facings and placement make a difference: See P. Chandon, J. W. Hutchinson, E. T. Bradlow, and S. H. Young, "Does In-Store Marketing Work? Effects of the Number and Position of Shelf Facings on Brand Attention and Evaluation at the Point of Purchase," *Journal of Marketing* 73, no. 6 (2009): 1–17.

95 Kathleen Sebelius: See K. Sebelius, mHealth Summit keynote address, December 5, 2011, http://www.fiercehealthit.com/press-release /mhealth-summit-speech-kathleen-sebelius.

95 Topol's view of the brave new world of mobile health: The quotes from Drs. Eric Topol and Nancy Snyderman come from her television interview of him on NBC News, January 24, 2013, "The Key to Better Health Care May Already Be in Your Pocket . . . and It's Not Your Wallet," http://rockcenter.nbcnews.com/_news/2013/01/24/16677207-the -key-to-better-health-care-may-already-be-in-your-pocket-and-its-not -your-wallet. For a deeper take on Topol's beliefs about how the smartphone will revolutionize medicine, see his book *The Patient Will See You Now* (New York: Basic Books, 2015).

96 whether early diagnosis of problems . . . is a good thing: Dr. Welch has produced an impressive body of work illuminating the very real problems of overtesting and overdiagnosis. Much of the problem is due to the failure to evaluate screening tests using randomized controlled trials; this can lead to misplaced beliefs about how well the screening tests are performing. For example, suppose our measure of success is how long patients survive once they are diagnosed with a disease. Earlier testing may catch a disease earlier in its course, but the time from diagnosis to death will by definition increase even if earlier diagnosis doesn't lead to more effective treatment. For an accessible review of this and other problems, see H. G. Welch, L. Schwartz, and S. Woloshin, *Overdiagnosed: Making People Sick in the Pursuit of Health* (Boston: Beacon Press, 2011).

**CHAPTER 7. REFRAME THE CHOICES**

106 it's not what you say that counts: For more wisdom on framing and

communication, see F. I. Luntz, *Words That Work: It's Not What You Say, It's What People Hear* (New York: Hyperion, 2007). George Lakoff's *Moral Politics: How Liberals and Conservatives Think* (Chicago: University of Chicago Press, 2002) offers a view from the other side of the political aisle about the importance of framing.

109  One way to reframe choices is to use social norms: Goldstein's hotel towel study is reported in N. J. Goldstein, R. B. Cialdini, and V. Griskevicius, "A Room with a Viewpoint: Using Social Norms to Motivate Environmental Conservation in Hotels," *Journal of Consumer Research* 35, no. 3 (2008): 472–82. For more details on Ayres's study of the effect of social norms on energy use, see I. Ayres, S. Raseman, and A. Shih, "Evidence from Two Large Field Experiments That Peer Comparison Feedback Can Reduce Residential Energy Usage," National Bureau of Economic Research Working Paper 15386, September 2009, http://www.nber.org/papers/w15386. The Beshears study of the use of social norms to increase 401(k) participation (and how it backfired for some employees) is reported in J. Beshears, J. J. Choi, D. Laibson, B. C. Madrian, and K. L. Milkman, "The Effect of Providing Peer Information on Retirement Savings Decisions," RAND Working Paper WR-800-SSA, 2010, http://www.rand.org/pubs/working_papers/WR800.html. The "backfire" effect observed when using social norms to reduce energy use can be found in D. L. Costa and M. E. Kahn, "Energy Conservation 'Nudges' and Environmentalist Ideology: Evidence from a Randomized Residential Electricity Field Experiment," *Social Science Research Network*, April 2010, http://papers.ssrn.com/sol3/papers.cfm?abstract_id=1594573.

114  the curious "decoy" effect: For details on the study of the restaurant recommendation scenario described, see J. Huber, J. Payne, and C. Puto, "Adding Asymmetrically Dominated Alternatives: Violations of Regularity and the Similarity Hypothesis," *Journal of Consumer Research* 9, no. 1 (1982): 90–98. Although the decoy effect has been replicated in a number of other settings, the underlying mechanism remains unclear.

## CHAPTER 8. PIGGYBACK IT

120  "A Spoonful of Sugar": Richard Sherman recounts the story of this and other *Mary Poppins* songs in an interview with Josephine Reed of the National Endowment for the Arts. You can hear it at http://arts.gov/sites/default/files/Sherman-podcast.mp3.

121  By carefully positioning the targets: Richard Thaler and Cass Sunstein explain the "fly in the urinal" application and report on its effectiveness

in preventing overspray in their book *Nudge: Improving Decisions About Health, Wealth, and Happiness* (New Haven: Yale University Press, 2008).

124 a side effect of playing the lottery: The study of using a lottery to help patients be more adherent to their blood-thinning medications is reported in S. E. Kimmel, A. B. Troxel, G. Loewenstein, A. B. Troxel, C. M. Brensinger, J. Jaskowiak, J. A. Doshi, M. Laskin, and K. Volpp, "Randomized Trial of Lottery-Based Incentives to Improve Warfarin Adherence," *American Heart Journal* 164, no. 2 (2012): 268–74. Details of the weight-loss studies can be found in K. G. Volpp, L. K. John, A. B. Troxel, L. Norton, J. Fassbender, and G. Loewenstein, "Financial Incentive-Based Approaches for Weight Loss: A Randomized Trial," *Journal of the American Medical Association* 300, no. 22 (2008): 2631–37; and in L. K. John, G. Loewenstein, A. B. Troxel, L. Norton, J. E. Fassbender, and K. G. Volpp, "Financial Incentives for Extended Weight Loss: A Randomized, Controlled Trial," *Journal of General Internal Medicine* 26, no. 6 (2011) 621–26.

## CHAPTER 9. SIMPLIFY WISELY

129 Barack Obama trailed Jon Stewart . . . in the polls: When *Parade.com*'s "PopCulture Summer Survey" of 2008 pitted Senator Obama against television's Jon Stewart, Stewart took 55 percent of the vote (see http://blogs.reuters.com/world-wrap/2008/07/11 /shocker-simon-cowell-most-obnoxious-celeb-paradecom/).

130 Wayne Gerdes took the top honors: The inaugural World Fuel Economy Championship was a bit of a grassroots affair, with the results posted on an online fuel economy forum (see http://www.cleanmpg.com/forums /showthread.php?t=12620).

130 *hypermiling* . . . was selected best new word of the year: See Oxford University Press's blog entry announcing the word of the year for 2008 at http://blog.oup.com/2008/11/hypermiling/.

130 sales of hybrid vehicles: Reported sales of hybrids were obtained from Hybridcars.com's "Market Dashboard." April 2008 figures were from http://www.hybridcars.com/april-2008-hybrids-defy-recession/; May 2007 sales were from http://www.hybridcars.com/may07-overview/.

132 our focus on miles per gallon . . . misdirects our attention: The study of the MPG metric and the computational errors it can cause is reported in R. P. Larrick and J. B. Soll, " The MPG Illusion," *Science* 320, no. 5583 (2008): 1593–94.

135 all they had to do was check a box: For details about how Laibson and colleagues used simplification to increase enrollment in 401(k) plans, see

J. Beshears, J. J. Choi, D. Laibson, and B. C. Madrian, "Simplification and Saving," *Journal of Economic Behavior & Organization* 95 (November 2013): 130–45 (also available at the National Bureau of Economic Research's website at http://www.nber.org/papers/w12659).

136 neuroscientists and psychologists refer to it as *fluency:* For a nice summary of this topic, see D. M. Oppenheimer, "The Secret Life of Fluency," *Trends in Cognitive Science* 12, no. 6 (2008): 237–41.

136 It's possible to alter fluency: For the study on the effects fonts have on perceptions of cities, see A. L. Alter and D. M. Oppenheimer, "Effects of Fluency on Psychological Distance and Mental Construal (or Why New York Is a Large City, but New York Is a Civilized Jungle)," *Psychological Science* 19, no. 2 (2008): 161–67. Alter and Oppenheimer also did the study on how we judge the value of foreign versus familiar currency: A. L. Alter and D. M. Oppenheimer, "Easy on the Mind, Easy on the Wallet: The Roles of Familiarity and Processing Fluency in Valuation Judgments," *Psychonomic Bulletin & Review* 15, no. 5 (2008): 985–90.

136 Fluency can also be affected by the names we give things: For the effect of how ticker symbols may affect a stock's performance on the day the company goes public, see A. L. Alter and D. M. Oppenheimer, "Predicting Short-Term Stock Fluctuations by Using Processing Fluency," *Proceedings of the National Academy of Science* 103, no. 24 (2006): 9369–72. The study of the association between font legibility and judgments about how long it takes to prepare an unfamiliar recipe is reported in H. Song and N. Schwarz, "If It's Hard to Read, It's Hard to Do: Processing Fluency Affects Effort Prediction and Motivation," *Psychological Science* 19, no. 10 (2008): 986–88. For the study demonstrating that roller coasters with names that are more difficult to pronounce are perceived as being riskier, see H. Song and N. Schwarz, "If It's Difficult to Pronounce, It Must Be Risky," *Psychological Science* 20, no. 2 (2009): 135–38.

137 you may be better off making *all* of the choices *more* difficult: The "Moses and the Ark" and "Louis Armstrong moon quote" studies are reported in T. D. Erickson and M. E. Mattson, "From Words to Meaning: A Semantic Illusion," *Journal of Verbal Learning and Verbal Behavior* 20, no. 5 (1981): 540–51; and M. Shafto and D. G. MacKay, "The Moses, Mega-Moses, and Armstrong Illusions: Integrating Language Comprehension and Semantic Memory," *Psychological Science* 11, no. 5 (2000): 372–78. For more detail about how making the "trick" questions harder to read increases the rate at which people answer correctly, see H. Song and N. Schwarz, "Fluency and the Detection of Misleading Questions: Low Processing

Fluency Attenuates the Moses Illusion," *Social Cognition* 26, no. 6 (2008): 791–99.

### CHAPTER 10. FORGING A NEW SCIENCE FOR BETTER BEHAVIOR

143 unintended pregnancies . . . come at a heavy cost: For an overview of the magnitude of this problem, see A. Sonfield, "What Women Already Know: Documenting the Social and Economic Benefits of Family Planning," Guttmacher Policy Review, Winter 2013, https://www .guttmacher.org/pubs/gpr/16/1/gpr160108.html; and Guttmacher Institute, "Fact Sheet: Unintended Pregnancy in the United States," Guttmacher Institute, February 2015, http://www.guttmacher.org/pubs/FB -Unintended-Pregnancy-US.html.

144 removing the cost barrier isn't enough: Results from Family PACT are reported in D. G. Foster, M. A. Biggs, J. Malvin, M. Bradsberry, P. Darney, and C. D. Brindis, "Cost-Savings from the Provision of Specific Contraceptive Methods in 2009," *Women's Health Issues* 23, no. 4 (2013): e265–e271. A comparison of contraceptive claims data following the implementation of the contraceptive mandate in the ACA to similar time periods prior to its implementation showed little difference in the prevalence of use of LARC methods in a very large commercially insured population (personal communication from S. Frazee, August 18, 2014).

146 CHOICE used tiered counseling: For more information about how CHOICE Project staff counseled participants, see G. M. Secura, J. E. Allsworth, T. Madden, J. L. Mullersman, and J. F. Peipert, "The Contraceptive CHOICE Project: Reducing Barriers to Long-Acting Reversible Contraception," *American Journal of Obstetrics and Gynecology* 203, no. 2 (2010): 115.e1–115.e7; and T. Madden, J. L. Mullersman, K. J. Omvig, G. M. Secura, and J. F. Peipert, "Structured Contraceptive Counseling Provided by the Contraceptive CHOICE Project," *Contraception* 88, no. 2 (2013): 243–49.

147 in-home tests for sexually transmitted infections: A randomized controlled trial by the CHOICE staff proved that this approach significantly improved performance; see A. S. Graseck, G. M. Secura, J. E. Allsworth, T. Madden, and J. F. Peipert, "Home Screening Compared with Clinic-Based Screening for Sexually Transmitted Infections," *Obstetrics & Gynecology* 115, no. 4 (2010) 745–52.

148 CHOICE's application of these fifty bits strategies is jaw-dropping: See G. M. Secura, T. Madden, C. McNicholas, J. Mullersman, C. Buckel, Q. Zhao, and J. F. Peipert, "Provision of No-Cost, Long-Acting Contraception and Teenage Pregnancy," *New England Journal of Medicine* 371, no. 14 (2014): 1316–23.

# Index

NOTE: Page numbers in *italics* indicate exhibits (data).

# About the Author

BOB NEASE, PhD, served as the chief scientist of Express Scripts and is the author of more than seventy peer-reviewed papers. He was also an associate professor of internal medicine at Washington University in St. Louis and an assistant professor at the Geisel School of Medicine at Dartmouth College. He received the Henry Christian Award for Excellence in Research from the American Federation for Medical Research and the URAC's Health Care Consumer Empowerment and Protection Award. He and his wife currently divide their time between Phoenix, Austin, and Italy.